HIDDEN TREASURE

HIDDEN TREASURE

A Journey Towards Healing from Sexual Abuse

Muriel Green and Anne Townsend

DARTON·LONGMAN+TODD

First published 1994 by
Darton, Longman and Todd Ltd
1 Spencer Court
140–142 Wandsworth High Street
London SW18 4JJ

ISBN 0–232–52003–8

A catalogue record for this book is available
from the British Library

Thanks are due to Faber and Faber Ltd for permission to quote from
The Elder Statesman by T. S. Eliot

Poems by Maggie Tulliver are from *A Restoration in Time*, published
privately by Kingfisher Design Services, London NW2.
Tel: 081–444 4666. © Kingfisher
Design, Maggie Tulliver 1992. Reproduced by permission.

Phototypeset by Intype, London
Printed and bound in Great Britain
at the University Press, Cambridge

CONTENTS

1

DISCOVERING OURSELVES

We eyed one another, half in trust and half in suspicion. Each of us had been hurt by other people just like us, by well-meaning Christian people who came from the backgrounds from which we came. We recognized our vulnerability and yet we sensed an inevitability about this particular meeting. Were we going to have enough courage to share ourselves with the kind of honesty that strips off protective pretences but which threatened to leave us exposed and open to misinterpretation?

It was about fifteen years since we had last been together but it felt more like fifteen hundred years. We had both changed inwardly out of all recognition during that time. Our acquaintance had first begun when we both worked overseas as missionaries sponsored by the same large, popular evangelical London church. We had met from time to time when on leave, usually on platforms, publicly to share at church meetings the goodness of God in our different spheres of work – Muriel as the Personnel Director of a relief and development project in Bangladesh sponsored by TEAR Fund (The Evangelical Alliance Relief Fund) and Anne as a missionary doctor in Thailand working with the Overseas Missionary Fellowship. Those had been the days when our success as missionaries had been intoxicating, and the sharing of stories of joy and of achievement on the 'mission field' was expected from us. We obliged by selecting and sharing the stories we thought our listeners wanted to hear. We painted idealistic pictures of our lives, of the way in which God faithfully answered our prayers and those of our church, and we barely allowed ourselves a cursory glimpse in the direction of the uncomfortable stirrings within our innermost selves which urged us to explore and to think more deeply, with less passive acceptance, about the faith which had led us overseas as missionaries.

Our misgivings about our meeting after so many years proved groundless. We looked long and hard at one another – noting time's obvious changes: the new facial furrows, the grey hairs and, with relief, the hoped-for deepened empathy. Each of us felt, 'I think I can trust her!' and our stories began to tumble off our lips and into the heart of the other.

Both of us had lived through the kind of crisis of faith which we had naively assumed would have been impossible for us to face in our heady missionary days when we blithely went along with sayings like: 'God's in heaven and all's right with the world.' The blow had come for both of us when we had no longer felt that God was in heaven – or even that God existed – and there was so much wrong in our personal inner worlds that God seemed irrelevant and impotent. We shared our stories of loss of faith. We talked about the pain and hurt, of the darkness of feeling God's apparent abandonment – darkness in which we had not been snuffed out but in which we could discover no lights to guide our faltering steps.

For Anne, the crisis had come when she could no longer endure a state of affairs which was turning into an increasingly impossible compromise of her integrity. Being in full-time Christian work, and finding that she no longer subscribed to all she had once believed, she felt trapped and desperate. After months of struggle, feeling caught in a web that would trap her for life, she tried to take her life – and failed. This was followed by months of what can be described simply and vaguely as a 'nervous breakdown'. Then came several rich and healing years of psychotherapy in which Anne diced with God, didn't lose, and discovered God to be different (far greater and more unpredictable) from the God she had once known. From here her journey took her into training as a counsellor, training for ministry as a clergy-person in the Church of England, then into work as a hospital chaplain and then herself to train as a psychotherapist.

Muriel's loss of God was rooted elsewhere. It was as a missionary that the first unwelcome questions and stirrings of doubt began to haunt her. She had gone to Bangladesh for an initial period of three years but with a lifetime commitment in mind. This made it particularly difficult when chronic gut problems brought her back home early – knowing that on medical grounds she could never go back. On returning to the United Kingdom with her missionary career in tatters and feeling an utter failure, the defences supporting her inner world began to erode within her. God seemed no longer to be a rock on which to build her life but rather to be the kind of sinking sand which would submerge and engulf her sense of lostness.

Tentative attempts to express her pain were not heard and at that time it seemed to Muriel that no one could understand or accept a Christian worker like her who could apparently be filled with doubt and despair – instead of being the shining example to others that she was supposed to be.

The fear of earning disapproval and the need to conform to the expectations of others was too great and Muriel did with her Bangladesh experience what she had always done with other painful memories – buried it and tried to erase it from memory as though it hadn't really happened. But, as she was to discover, it was buried alive and festered away until four and a half years later it erupted in the form of deep depression. She could no longer hide the fact that her inner experience matched neither her own outer experiences of faith nor the expectations of others.

Pastoral care was of limited help for, again, few people understood her inner turmoil or seemed able to accept that Christians and ex-missionaries could apparently disintegrate spiritually and emotionally as she seemed to be doing – it seemed to them that she was obviously 'backsliding'. Her sense of rejection by the Church and by her friends was enormous.

The turning point came when her pastor, finding himself out of his depth, put Muriel in touch with Care and Counsel and the ensuing brief period of crisis counselling which followed was her introduction to a process that would, over the years, prove to be painful, liberating and life-transforming.

However, it was not until two years later, when Muriel found a psychotherapist to whom she could unfold her story, that she was able to begin to acknowledge her sense of abandonment by God and her spiritual desolation. This was the start of her journey of discovery and exploration, of pain and growth, which has resulted in a deep and honest, intensely personal inner experience of God and which has gone on to take her into training as a counsellor.

As we shared the story of our journeys away from the certainties we had experienced at the fundamentalist end of evangelicalism, we recognized in each other kindred spirits. Such recognition was warm and nourishing, for both of us had felt the cold winds of rejection and criticism from some of our Christian friends of the past. We were learning that it was all right with God for us to be different from the people we once had been, that it was Christian growth (not – as some suggested – disobedience to God) that had led us to embark on journeys with far fewer certain guidelines than had been ours in the past. Although it was all right with God, we were aware that this was not so for some of our Christian friends. We felt uncomfortable in the presence of those who branded us as 'backsliders' and then wrote us off as being a potential danger to the faith of others.

Our susceptibility to needing to conform to the known wishes and beliefs of religious authority made our being different from the people we had been in the past painful. We wanted to be accepted and to belong, so feelings and fear of rejection hurt. We were relieved to find in one another a similarity in the pattern our pathways had taken over the past few years. Where once we had accepted the blackness and whiteness of our fundamentalist Christian position, we were learning to live comfortably with the greyness of not always possessing easy answers to hard questions. We were learning that to be a Christian agnostic, to give the answer 'I don't know', was vital to our integrity at that time. What 'authority' thought about us still mattered, but its power was weakening and its stranglehold diminished.

Our discovery that we had one more thing in common surprised, humbled and delighted us. We found that for both of us, the subject of sexual abuse was one that was increasingly important to us. It seemed to Anne that the subject had been thrust upon her. In the course of counsellor training, she had sat through sessions in which two people had disclosed their abuse for the very first time. To her amazement, she survived listening, and found that the subject moved and angered her and spurred her into action. Later on, in the course of counselling work, several women found their way to Anne's consulting room wanting support as they began to confront their past stories of childhood abuse. A nucleus of Christians who had been abused came into her orbit and she and a colleague invited them to meet one another for a day to talk about the ways in which their Christianity had been affected by their experiences. This led to something bigger as about 100 people asked for similar days for themselves, and so every three to four months a day was run for about forty Christians (men and women, lay and ordained, from different denominations) who had survived abuse and wanted to study their experience from a Christian perspective.

For Muriel, abuse was less of an academic topic and more of a personal one. About fifteen months after beginning psychotherapy, acutely painful childhood memories began to surface of how she had been sexually abused by the baby-sitter while her parents were out at church meetings. In the months and years that followed she began to confront this issue in psychotherapy and to work through some of the effects it had had on her throughout her life.

By the time we met, both of us had begun to discover God in a fresh, vital and relevant way. We tried to integrate our perceptions and feelings about sexual abuse with our new insights about God. This was liberating and encouraging. Perhaps at that first meeting, a seed was sown in our hearts – we had discovered there was more to Christianity than we had previously realized and that this spoke into our understanding of sexual abuse. Perhaps we had something we might offer to others in the form of a book.

Like others, we had become increasingly aware that the sexual abuse of children (and adults) was far more common than previously realized. Figures of known occurrences vary. Statistics are difficult to collect but a survey in East Anglia in the 1980s suggested that one in every six women and one in every eight men was the victim of sexual abuse of one kind or another in childhood. Of the perpetrators, 96 per cent were male and 4 per cent were female. Of the mothers of those who were abused, 80 per cent had been victims of childhood abuse themselves.

Ray Wyre, the Director of the Gracewell Clinic (one of the few treatment centres for sex offenders) is reported in *The Lancet*[1] as estimating that 'fixated paedophiles' on average abuse at least 100 children.

A MORI survey of 2,019 adults aged over fifteen in September 1984, on the basis of retrospective recall, showed that about one in ten had been sexually abused as children. Under-reporting is usual, although in Leeds writers in *The Lancet*[2] state that 'cases coming to our attention have risen from ten in 1983 to 106 in 1985 and were 104 in the first six months of 1986'. They add that they:

> Now see as many cases of sexual abuse as physical abuse in children in Leeds, and anorectal abuse of young children is more common than the battered child syndrome in this age group. Although recognized cases of all types of abuse, including fondling and touching, masturbation, child prostitution and pornography, and intercourse (oral, anal, and vaginal) have risen, we have become more aware of more cases of anal abuse than of any other forms of sexual abuse in very young children of both sexes.

And they write:

> Anal abuse in very young children frequently arises within the family. As our results show, the father or father figure is the most common perpetrator, although mothers may also abuse their children . . . there is little doubt that anal abuse is likely to lead to serious long-term emotional damage . . .

We were becoming increasingly aware of women and men who had been abused as children who now felt able to own their past and to seek help in working it through and in finding some degree of healing. It seemed to us that we had something special to offer through Muriel's story of her personal journey through abuse to find a measure of healing. We were well aware that finding a measure of healing after sexual abuse is a complicated and slow process but that it may be rendered even more complex for survivors who are Christians – especially those, like us, with a fairly black and white type of Christianity. We know some people, battered and bruised by their pasts, for whom a fundamentalist evangelical background has added even greater pressure as they struggle to make sense of the questions numbing, bombarding or overwhelming their inner selves. They often face questions like: 'Why did God let it happen? Where was God? Doesn't God love me enough to stop it?' and 'How can God be a father when my father abused me?' They are made to stumble by less than helpful comments from those Christians who tell them to 'rejoice in the Lord always!' and state categorically that 'all things work together for good to them that love God!' and that 'God will give you a rich and great ministry because of all the suffering he has entrusted to you!' In the face of such apparently callous dogmatism, some find it impossible and too risky to confront the questions they need to ask if they are not to be hypocrites wearing masks declaring them to be other than the hurting and vulnerable people they really are.

Our personal experiences showed that questioning was difficult and risky for us in the days when we lined ourselves up in the evangelical Christian position. We both found that people from other wings of the Church were more willing and able to hear us, less defensive and threatened by our words and more tolerant of our need to question and our need, for a time, to deny our faith. Our journeys towards healing and richer faith have included periods of dark despair softened and lightened by healing moments when suddenly we were able to be in touch with the feelings associated with all our doubts and fears, with our questions, and with all the bottled up anger directed at God.

Both of us (on our separate but parallel journeys) slowly realized that God does not say that he will accept us only when we have finally resolved all our doubts and fears. God is not saying 'Come to me and all your problems will melt away!' Rather God invites us to 'come' with all our fears and doubts. We are to 'come' in spite of them.

Our experience suggests that evangelicalism is often presented as a faith that guarantees freedom from fear. And yet, many evangelical Christians seem to be bound by fear. We have been in situations in which it seemed too risky to

allow freedom to ask questions, to put faith under a micro-
scope, to express doubts and worries, or even to turn one's
back on faith or on God when neither seemed to make
sense any more. We know Christians who have lost their
former naive faith either temporarily or permanently and,
as a result, stand condemned by others for having 'backslid-
den'. It seems impossible for some Christians to trust God
to be responsible for the spiritual journey of another person
– they need to interfere with that person, assume parental
responsibility and tell the other what to do and what not to
do.

Pressure may be brought to bear on the 'doubter' in words
like: 'God loves you. If only you trust him more your scars
and hurts from your past will disappear.' 'If only you had
more faith then God would be able to heal your wounds.'
'Jesus is all you need for everything. The Bible says, "God
will supply all your needs" and so you must appropriate all
that is already available to you in God.' Or 'The Bible says
"All things work together for good . . ." and God wants to
use your experience for the good of others so you should
stop being selfish and think about others who are worse off
than you.' 'If you pray and read your Bible regularly then
everything will be all right.' And 'memories from your past
can be healed once and for all if you pray this special prayer
and trust God in this way . . .' The list is endless . . .

But the question arises: What happens to those of us
whose experience cannot match such huge and subtle
expectations from others? Suppose our faith is dimly flickering and we cannot fan the flame enough to have the kind
of trust that others tell us will revolutionize our inner selves?
Are we doomed to despair and failure? Is it all our fault for
being so ineffective and impotent?

Supposing we hear other Christians claiming that their
particular way of following God is the way – the only way –
in which we are to live if we are to be 'successful' Christians?
What happens if our personal experience indicates that their
way doesn't work for us? Is there something wrong with us?

Many Christian victims of sexual abuse face dilemmas
like these. They are caught in the fear-filled contradiction
between the way in which their church, their Christian
friends, or certain Christian counsellors say Christianity

works or does not work. They are told their spiritual lives should/ought/could or might follow a certain pattern. But they find that they are different. The should's, ought's and must's seem unattainable. It is in ways like this that certain forms of Christianity may compound the damage already caused by abuse.

We long for Christians and for churches to be more open, to understand and empathize with the subject. We beg you to:

- Take off your blinkers and open your eyes to see what is going on around you. Our personal experience enables us to state that abuse does occur in Christian families and in churches. Abusers known to us include those who appear to be pillars of the Church – such as clergymen, priests, youth leaders, evangelists and administrators.

- Open your ears to listen and to hear non-judgementally, uncritically, with acceptance and empathy. Abused people may have tried (often as children) to test-share their stories, only to find that they are not believed. If you are in the privileged position of being entrusted with someone's story, then honour that trust, for the risk in telling is great and the expectation on the part of the one who shares with you may well be that you will not hear and believe.

- Open your minds and hearts to the fact that we, Christians, do not have all the answers for sexual abuse survivors. We do not have a monopoly of the truth. We cannot prescribe one particular pathway which guarantees healing, for the outworking of God's loving integrating power is as diverse as there are people in the world.

- Open your minds to accept the fact that survivors of abuse often have to ask uncomfortable and disturbing questions. They need permission to express anger, and often need to reject God and their faith because they sense they have been betrayed by God. This is often the necessary stepping stone across a gulf and back finally to encounter God again.

- Let go of your self-sufficiency as a Christian – for most survivors will require professional counselling or therapy outside of the Church. There is a lot of suspicion within

some parts of the evangelical world towards psychotherapy – through a well-meaning but misguided belief
that it is guaranteed to destroy faith. Our own years of
being in psychotherapy have offered us some of our
greatest achievements, and rather than damaging our
faith we now have a deeper experience of God than we
had before.

Christians who have been sexually abused face their own
special problems. One of our friends, Maggie, shared her
feelings of having been used sexually as a child in the context of a Christian home, in this poetic parable about the
'pharisee' who abused her:

> I was twelve years old and
> the day was hot and the atmosphere inside the house
>   was stifling.
> My father had actually only invited his Pharisee friends
> and his new friend, Jesus.
> But word got around
> and the food we had prepared
> for what should have been a handful of guests
> was woefully inadequate for the fifty or so
> crammed into the living room.
> As the younger daughter of the house,
> I was to have passed the food around.
> I was curious to see Jesus so close
> but the anticipation had been spoiled
> by the knowledge that *he* was coming.
> He came too often, my father's friend, the Pharisee,
> and every time he came, he would find occasion to touch
>   me –
> only a fumble or a fondle through my clothes
> but I dreaded his visits.
> And then *he* spoke up.
> 'Who can forgive sins but God alone?'
> I couldn't believe my ears.
> Why this sudden concern about sin, I thought bitterly . . .
> and the word hypocrite went through and through my
>   head.
> Who was *he* to pretend to be so pure –

or didn't he ever put the words beside the deeds,
the sins done against me?

The horror of Maggie's abuse has been something with which she has struggled for the last thirty years. She, unlike many others, has been able to find a measure of healing of body, mind and spirit, and shares her experience of God meeting her in prayer one day:

> . . . and there was Jesus putting his arm around me.
> My tears were shaking me but I didn't need to say
>   anything.
> 'I know,' he said, 'It's all right,' again and again, his
> strong arm telling me that it was all right.
> 'But what about *him*?' I managed.
> The reply came without hesitation, 'That's not your
> responsibility. His double standard is something for me
>   and him to work out.
> You can leave that one with me.' And as I sat there,
>   oblivious of all else, the tears subsided and the joy
>   began to rise and with it a sure knowledge of cleansing
>   healing.

We have written this book to share our experience of healing with those of you who are survivors yourself, and also to share with others of you who want to understand more about finding healing after the trauma of sexual abuse.

2

A MATTER OF FACTS

'I'd never have thought something like that could happen in our family – it's such a loving one and we all get on so well together!' wept Joan, Pete's mother, typical of a sad number of parents, relatives and friends who unknowingly collude with the fact that sexual abuse is occurring within a particular family set-up.

Because more often than not the perpetrator of child sexual abuse is a family member or a trusted family friend, the problem of disbelief is further compounded. 'Not us . . . that sort of thing happens in other families!' is the typical response. Quite often the abuse is 'known about' at an unconscious level by several family members and even by friends. Warning signs may be passed off, ignored, repressed or denied as being of no significance, so that years later Joan confessed through tear-filled eyes:

> Yes! Now I see why it was that Pete was so quiet and subdued after those long sessions he had with his Dad in the study – but I'd assumed they were sharing and praying together, as father and son should do, and so I never interrupted them and thought no more of it.

She had even managed to ignore the fact that bed-wetting in Pete's case had continued well into his teens, and had effortlessly silenced the commonsense part of her which knew perfectly well that bed-wetting so late on was far from usual and that her other children had been dry from a very young age. It was only when Pete confronted his Dad (when his father was in his 60s) and his father denied the abuse, that certain events and family secrets fell into place for Joan and she could see with horrible clarity what had been taking place all those years in their apparently 'happy Christian family' home. She was aghast and overwhelmed by guilt at her blindness and deafness to her son's childhood plight. She found it hard to understand how much fear her gentle vicar husband had engendered in Pete about the terrible consequences which would ensue should he ever talk about the sexual abuse that had taken place day after day in the supposedly carefree school holidays.

Sadly, sexual abuse is far more common than most people realize. We hold the view that sexual abuse of children is any action by any adult that uses any child to meet the sexual/emotional needs of an adult. Tragically it occurs within the orbit of the Church and within committed Christian families far more than had been anticipated, as well as outside them. Dr Arnon Bentovim, a Consultant Psychiatrist at Great Ormond Street Hospital, uses this definition to explain what sexual abuse is. He suggests that:

> Child sexual abuse is the involvement of dependent, developmentally immature children and adolescents in sexual activity they do not truly comprehend, to which they are unable to give informed consent and which violates the social taboos of family roles.[1]

He says that the following can come into the category of being sexual abuse: pseudo-educational contact; fondling of genitals; masturbation of child; masturbation of adult; oral or genital contact; simulated sexual intercourse; vaginal intercourse; anal intercourse; plus all forms of inappropriate sexualized contact with a child; plus child pornography; plus child prostitution.

We believe that there are no degrees of abuse. All abuse is abuse and abuse is serious. Our experience is that one incident of inappropriate touching can be as traumatic for one vulnerable person as years of genital stimulation or penetrative abuse may be for another. There would seem, however, to be degrees of trauma and damage the extent of which will depend on factors like: the closeness of the relationship between the abuser and the victim; the personality of the victim; how often the abuse occurred; the period of time over which the abuse took place; what sort of abuse occurred; what sort of response the victim received when he or she tried to tell. It is important, therefore, to take each victim of abuse as they are and to accept that the damage from their abuse is as it is experienced and described by that person and never to make hasty judgements based on preconceived ideas about how serious the damage 'should' or 'should not' be.

Yet, we hear all kinds of justifications being made for this – some more plausible than others and some containing half-truths or truths that are twisted to suit the speaker. We hear words like: 'It's all part of growing up . . .', 'It's best for children to learn by seeing and doing . . .', 'There's no harm in something as natural as this . . .'. These are some of the reasons adults put forward to try to make acceptable the kind of sexual experience that they may give children before those children have reached an age when they are ready to learn intimate details about sexual activity in their own bodies. Our sad experience is that this may, and does at times, occur within what should be a very safe arena – namely that of a church fellowship or other Christian context. Sometimes this exposure is gross and obviously out of order, while at other times it is more subtle.

It is easy to condemn the leader of a boy's houseparty who crept into Tom's tent one night and began to fondle him sexually – culminating after ten days with both Tom's professed conversion to Christianity and with the perpetration of anal intercourse. Talking to Tom as an adult Christian leader now in mid-life we are saddened by the traumatic and dehumanizing effect this has had both on him as a person made in the image of God and on the kind of Christianity he now practices. It is less easy to judge the motives of some of those adults who find (acknowledged or hidden) sexual gratification in showing explicit sex education films to their youth groups – for adults differ in the conscious and unconscious reasons as to why they show such material to young people and may have no overt or hidden motives that would be harmful to a youngster. However, we have come across instances where 'in the name of Christ' material has been shown to the young that has been harmful to some, and has gone against the interests of the children watching it, but has served the sexual needs of the person showing the material.

Some people may not realize that what happened to them

as children was in fact sexual abuse. We would suggest that any one of the following might indicate sexual abuse: being touched in sexual areas; being shown a sexual film or forced to listen to sexual talk; being made to pose for seductive or sexual photographs; being subjected to unnecessary intimate medical treatment in the bikini area; being forced to perform oral sex with an adult or sibling; being raped or otherwise penetrated; being fondled, kissed, or held in a way that felt uncomfortable; being forced to take part in ritualized abuse in which there was physical or sexual torture; being made to watch or look at sexual parts; being bathed in a way that felt intrusive; being ridiculed about your body; being encouraged or goaded into sex you didn't really want; being told that 'all you are good for is sex', and being involved in child prostitution or pornography.

It is obvious that children need protecting from risk, and current legislation, in the form of The Children's Act, tries to ensure that this is enforced in young people's activities within the Church as well as outside it. Recently (to the shame and embarrassment of many on the periphery and not directly involved in the situation) there have been instances where youth leaders working within a church context have been taken to court and prosecuted for inappropriate sexual activity with their charges. It is our experience however that abuse does not apply simply to children but that vulnerable adults are not always guaranteed the immunity they expect to find within a church fellowship from the kind of sexual exposure they would prefer to avoid or even find repelling. Such sexual involvement may include obvious sexual misconduct, sexual exploitation, sexual boundary violation and undue familiarity. It may range from a sermon which is just too sexually explicit for some members of the congregation or staff team and which leaves them feeling vaguely uncomfortable, to very intimate hugging and kissing, to someone with pastoral responsibility engaging in some kind of sexual activity with a member of the congregation for whom he (or she) is responsible. We are using the word 'he' since the abuse of power in this way tends to be carried out by men but it can also involve women in responsible positions.

We also know of several women who have been enticed

into sexual activity with male church leaders who have claimed that it is done 'in the name of Christ' and that 'it is God's will' for them to be intimate sexually. Pam told us that after sexual intercourse she and her pastor both knelt down by the bed and asked for God's forgiveness, felt better about what they had done, and then next day repeated the act. This had gone on for several years.

Psychiatrist Peter Rutter[2] says that he found that sexual abuse was more common than he had expected in the 'forbidden zone', and that it involved those he would have assumed to be responsible care-givers. He defines the 'forbidden zone' as being:

> Sexual behaviour between a man and a woman who have a professional relationship based on trust, specifically when the man is the woman's doctor, psychotherapist, pastor, lawyer, teacher or workplace mentor.[3]

He writes about a fairly predictable pattern of relationship that typically takes place, and explains that:

> These highly eroticized entanglements can occur behind closed doors, in any relationship in which a woman entrusts important aspects of her physical, spiritual, psychological, or material welfare to a man who has power over her.

He adds that:

> The men who have sex with their female patients, clients, parishioners, students are not the obviously disturbed men who occasionally show up in the headlines. Instead they are accomplished professionals, admired community leaders, and respectable family men whose integrity we tend to take for granted. I can now see that sexual violation of trust is an epidemic, mainstream problem that re-enacts in the professional relationship a wider cultural power imbalance between men and women.

His words ring true to us for we believe that the role and status of women in many church institutions and organizations indicates that such a power imbalance exists which is more marked than in society at large. The Anglican and

Roman Catholic Churches, for instance, are among those few organizations not to have a functioning equal opportunities policy and to exclude women from high office. This power imbalance suggests (what may seem to be unthinkable and impossible for many Christians to believe could be the case) the possibility that women may even run a greater risk of sexual exploitation within the framework of a church group or para-church organization than outside it.

Peter Rutter's words may ring alarm bells for some well-meaning and genuinely kind Christian male leaders. He writes:

> To me, and to all men in power, the woman can easily become a sympathetic, wounded, vulnerable presence who admires and needs us in an especially feminine way. If we have been working together for some time, a familiarity and trust develops between us that starts to erode the boundaries of seemingly impersonal relationships. Whether they say so openly or not these women often convey their feeling that we are treating them far better than they ever dreamed a man could. As a result, we may find ourselves experiencing a closeness, a comfort, a sense of completeness with these women that we have long sought but rarely found; many of them begin to feel the same way about being with us.[4]

Both of us have worked with women who have felt close in various ways to the male leader of their organization, whose intimacy has been enhanced by a shared spirituality and prayer life but whose trust has then been betrayed by the leader's misuse of it, and who have been left hurt and wounded and unable to share their story with anyone because (as they see it) 'to tell anyone what had happened would not be to the glory of God and might be to the detriment of Christianity'. Thus silence has been golden but bought with thirty pieces of silver stuffed into the mouth of the woman, who has been left unable to seek the help she desperately needs to work through her emotional damage. Rutter's words fly in the face of those Christians who commonly protect their male leaders by saying: 'But the woman seduced him . . .', or 'It takes two to tango and she's bound to be partly responsible for it . . .'. We believe that it is the person with the power (the one in authority) who carries the responsibility for setting the boundaries and for protecting and safeguarding a relationship.

We agree with Peter Rutter when he states that:

> Any sexual behaviour by a man in power within what I define as the forbidden zone is inherently exploitative of a woman's trust. Because he is the keeper of that trust, it is the man's responsibility, no matter what the level of provocation or apparent consent by the woman, to assure that sexual behaviour does not take place.[5]

When such trust is betrayed Rutter believes that both parties are the losers for:

> The damage a man causes himself when he violates these boundaries is often elusive, because in the moment of forbidden sex he may be able to convince himself that he is satisfying a deeply felt need. Yet in the very act of exploiting the woman in order to feel more fully alive, he abandons the search for aliveness within himself. When a man's brief moment of forbidden sexual release is over, he is left with more emptiness than before . . . and he is in denial of his own psychological wounds.[6]

The results of such abuse vary from person to person, and vary at different times of life. Childhood and adult abuse profoundly affects the survivors but the results cannot be tidily systematized. Some adults experience a typical post-traumatic stress reaction. Some who were abused as children may re-experience the abuse by talking about it, by playing it out, by drawings and day-dreaming, by flashbacks, through nightmares, through inappropriate sexual activity, by having a fear of certain symbolic places, people and things. Others tend to distance themselves from what happened to them by avoiding certain people, places and things which are linked in some way to the abuse, and find themselves unwilling and unable to talk about the limited memory of the abuse they may have, while many others have no conscious memory of this part of their past. In some cases children may be more stimulated than is usual – they may have difficulty in falling and staying asleep, may be irritable, angry and aggressive, easily distracted, hyper-alert, anxious or readily startled.

Alice Miller[7] believes that children must be reared in an environment in which they can flourish and in which adults respect and protect them. When vital needs are 'frustrated and children are instead abused for the sake of the adults' needs . . . then their integrity will be lastingly impaired. The normal reaction to such injury should be anger and pain.' She explains that children in this kind of hurtful environment:

> Are forbidden to express their anger and since it would be unbearable to experience their pain all alone, they are compelled to suppress their feelings, repress their memory of the trauma, and idealise those guilty of the abuse. Later they will have no memory of what was done to them. Dissociated from their original cause, the feelings of anger, helplessness, despair, longing, anxiety, and pain will find expression in destructive acts against others . . . or against themselves.

This may have lasting consequences, as she continues: 'If these people become parents, they will then often direct acts of revenge for their mistreatment in childhood against their own children, whom they use as scapegoats.'

Sexual abuse has long-term traumatic effects on a child and on the adult who develops from that child. These persist and may be apparent in emotional, intellectual, and behavioural difficulties of greater or lesser severity. Factors like age when the abuse occurred, the extent of the abuse, and the relationship the child had to the abuser at that particular time of his or her development, are important in determining the long-term effects of the abuse. Personality disorders (which go on into adult life) may develop through the child's unconscious attempts at coping with what has happened to him or her.

As with any other traumatic experience, sexual abuse affects other parts of the life cycle. Thus a child who was abused will be affected in some way in adolescence and adulthood and this in turn will affect marriage and family life.

In 1983, research[8] into incest showed that 80 per cent of

the survivors questioned said that they had at some time searched for some kind of meaning, reason or way to make sense of their experience, even though it had ceased up to twenty years earlier. About 50 per cent said that they could make no sense of it and that the passage of time made things no clearer. Those finding some degree of meaning found a degree of comfort in this. The search for many took the form of attempting to make some kind of sense of the dynamics of what had happened – reminiscent of the concept familiar to medical people of 'working through a trauma'. Thus some Christian survivors may not only work through what happened to them, seeking to understand it, but may also want to give this part of their past significance and value in their present life. While this may be a good thing to do we are aware that it is open to potential violation by others with apparently well-meaning motives. We think of some Christians known to us who have written personal accounts or been filmed telling their stories of abuse who, it seems to us, have been abused again by those who want to use their story either to make money or to win converts to a certain brand of Christianity. This may give the survivor some kind of purpose and meaning for the abuse but the way in which it is done, used and even exploited can turn out to be a repeat of the abusive cycle. Hidden, unknown and unconscious, motivation needs watching in this area, for people who have been sexually abused are more likely than other people to find themselves in situations where they are being abused in some way or another, not realizing that an old familiar pattern is being repeated.

R. M. Stein[9] suggests that modern Western society lacks viable rituals and social ways of dealing with the incest taboo. Instead of it being dealt with at a conscious level of the mind it has generally been relegated to the realms of the unconscious, and this has resulted in our society fearing sexuality and the power of instincts in general rather than our fearing incest. Sadly, this has resulted in many thousands of survivors being unable to share their story of sexual abuse with another person and of finding the healing that is possible through doing this. Secrecy is a characteristic feature of abuse.

3

SECRET TRAP

Despite all the television and media publicity given to the subject of sexual abuse in the last fifteen years, a conspiracy of silence still tends to surround the subject. When, if ever, did you last hear a sermon relating to this particular abuse of power? We hazard a guess that you have never heard such a sermon, nor preached yourself, on this topic!

Society, the judiciary system, the Church, the medical and the caring professions still often manage to collude and conspire either to paper-over the subject or to whitewash the whole situation, whilst tending to find excuses for the perpetrator's actions, seeking extenuating circumstances or even blaming the victimized child for being so irresistibly seductive (at an age when the child may barely be out of nappies) that sexual abuse was asked for and an inevitable consequence of that child's existence.

By and large, ministers and church members find it almost impossible to believe that sexual abuse has happened or still goes on in some Christian families. We have heard clergy state dogmatically that they are convinced that there cannot be anyone in their congregation who has been abused. Yet, in a couple of instances, we have known of more than three people who are survivors in a church in which the minister has given just such an assurance. We find that quite often the stories of abuse shared with us by Christians are being told for the first time ever, for many have been unable to share with anyone in their church the fact that it was a church office bearer who used them sexually. In some cases these abusers are still at large, no one having the courage or the power to confront them, or they themselves are secretly longing for help to extricate themselves from their situation but are unaware of where it is safe to seek help in breaking free.

Sylvia tried to tell her church leadership team what the youth leader was doing to her but was sent away with an angry retort: 'You wicked girl, trying to bring dishonour on a wonderful man like him . . . you're making it up just to get extra attention . . . we don't really want you in this church if you're going round telling such dreadful lies.' This kind of attitude means that some survivors receive mixed messages. They may have heard: 'You've no need to feel guilty. You've done nothing about which to feel ashamed.' But disclosure of what happened may leave them feeling an object of shame. Words may be spoken which apparently confirm the myth festering within them that they must have been to blame in some way or another and are therefore guilty.

Such replies include thoughtless but well-meaning words like: 'Why stir it up now – it happened so long ago!', 'Isn't it best left alone now. Just forget it.' 'Bury it in the past where it belongs . . .', 'Was it really that bad?' and, 'Aren't you blowing it up out of all proportion . . .?'.

This theme of diminution has many different shapes and forms and makes it understandable that many survivors are fearful of revealing their past stories. The risk run is that of betrayal. Betrayal of innocence and betrayal of trust. Each time a survivor falteringly, and mustering much courage, tries to share what has happened and is met by a response that feels like disbelief or rejection, yet another betrayal takes place. Emotional wounds are laid open yet again and may take weeks, months or years to begin to heal over. But on those occasions when faltering disclosure is met with acceptance and understanding (the hearing of the disclosure may be costly and painful for the listener) healing can take place at its own gentle pace.

For a survivor to navigate the silent ocean of secrecy surrounding sexual abuse requires courage, for the seas of shame and guilt are uncharted, and the rocks and shallows unpredictable. And yet it is only as survivors are able to own their stories openly that healing can begin. Disclosure is rarely completed in a once-for-all telling but requires time in which memories are allowed to return and the story can be repeated over and over throughout the weeks, months or even years. This is not indulgence, wallowing or needless repetition of the past but is the very necessary exposure of the darkness of the past to the healing rays of daylight, sunshine and the objectivity of the 'here and now'.

Confiding their secrets about sexual abuse seems beyond the realms of possibility for many children. They have been warned of dire and terrifying consequences should they tell. This is the reason why many try to drop subtle hints which avoid spelling out the stark truth – hoping that parents and responsible adults will read between the lines, hear their unspoken pleas for protection and move into caring action.

Typical for many people is Muriel's experience. She remembers: "Once hooked by my abuser, my silence was ensured and as a child I was rendered too powerless by my fear of the threatened consequences to protest or to stop the abuse." Her abuser was the male family friend who had with apparent kindness offered to stay in with the children while their parents attended frequent church meetings. Muriel tried to find ways of getting her parents to register her terror of being left with this man, without spelling out what was happening and thus of running the greater risk of the unnamed, fearful consequences of telling clearly. So, she tried what she calls "ways of telling that were not actually telling. If I couldn't risk telling openly, then perhaps my message could be heard by some other means that would make them aware of what was happening. I used to say things like: 'I don't want to stay with him. Please take me with you . . .' Or again: 'I don't want you to go, please don't leave me . . .' But my words were interpreted by my parents at face value. I was gently chided: 'You'll be all right. He'll look after you, put you to bed and read you a story.'

"No one heard the message hidden behind the words I was too frightened to utter in their stark fearfulness. I could not say what I wanted to say: 'He'll do bad things to me again if you go and leave me!' His warnings as to what would happen should I say anything paralysed me into submissive silence and inner quaking horror.

"And so my inarticulate cries for help went unheard and unheeded. I was powerless to struggle against his adult power of manipulating circumstances to fit in with his plans, and his adult masculine strength, and became a passive participator in the horror he regularly forced on me.

"Once the pattern of secrecy was established and threats were used it was impossible for me to break free. Like others who have tried to tell openly or obliquely and have not been heard or believed, my inner damage was compounded. I became convinced that even if I were to tell no one would believe me. My situation became appalling. Which was worse: to remain abandoned in the fear and pain of the abuse, or to run the risk of rejection by unbelieving grown-ups? I find that as an adult I still face similar deep-seated fears. It must be worse for those for whom the perpetrator was a parent, for the extra risk run in telling is that a much loved and much hated father could be sent to prison and the family split up. For many such children there appears to be no choice – silence is the sole option.

"There was no escape for me. Objective outer reality was hard to hold on to and I became caught up in my own inner world of secret nameless fears and intense pain. Since no one noticed my distress I dealt with the horror of it all in the only way I knew, by finding my own inner anaesthetic, by blanking it all out from my conscious mind and pretending that it was not really happening. It was as in these words I wrote subsequently:

> In all of this the one thing I learned
> when you invaded my space
> was to leave my body on the bed,
> escape in my mind to a safer place
> trying to find a way to efface
> and blank out the whole event."

It is easy to engage little children in the fun of having secrets 'just between the two of us' for secrets and childhood tend to go hand-in-hand and it is that which may be forbidden which often appears to be the most attractive. 'It's our special, private secret, so promise not to tell anyone else!' is a subtle and clever way of getting a child to acquiesce to silence about sexual abuse.

However, the power of the secrecy surrounding sexual abuse tends to be more sinister than the keeping of mere childish secrets. This particular secret behaviour takes place behind closed (or even locked) doors, often in darkness, is instinctively and quickly perceived by the child to be something of which parents would not approve, and may then be accompanied by dire threats of what will happen should the secret ever be discovered. A child's words: 'I'm frightened . . . I want to tell my Mummy . . .' are likely to be followed by all kinds of threats as to what will happen should parental figures be told about the secret. The child may face threats of physical violence, verbal abuse, a pet being harmed, a toy being destroyed, being locked away in a frightening place, being deprived of pleasure or of having pain forced on him or her.

For Muriel the threats "were all to do with my family and with loss. He whispered that Mummy and Daddy would say I was a bad girl and would be sure to punish me – Daddy was always ready to punish any infringement of family rules. My abuser said that my parents would stop loving me, that they wouldn't believe what I told them, and, worst of all, that it would kill my mother if she knew and then there wouldn't be anyone to look after us. I believed him and was terrified. I was only eight years old, shy and sensitive and very aware that my parents' marriage was under some stress. I was prepared to suffer anything to preserve the precarious balance of love and security in the family. He knew just where I was most vulnerable and aimed his threats in that direction – quickly hooking me into co-operating with his demands for total secrecy about 'our little game'."

Secrecy may not appear to some of us to be something that is very important. In fact, such secrecy forced onto little children can have the effect of stunting emotional growth and hindering the development of normal adult maturity and trust.

The damage caused by enforced secrecy about sexual abuse is crucial. It is closely linked with fear, and feelings of abandonment and rejection. For a child in whom these feelings are realized, the resulting emotional damage is compounded by feelings of desperate isolation, guilt and shame.

But finding words and language in which a child can share the unshareable and be believed often seems impossible. Muriel explains how hard it is for her, even now, to share what happened to her in the past, despite the fact that she is now an adult and no longer a child at the mercy of the adult world. Like many others, the grip that so many years of fear-filled secrecy have had on her is costly and traumatic to break in mid-life.

"I find I have this dilemma: How will people perceive
the reason I write of my abuse?
How will it be received?
I fear some will think it self-glory,
or seeking publicity.
That people won't see from my story
it's the only way to be free.
For when threatened by our abuser
if 'our secret' we should tell,
we learn to be silent through terror,
a lesson we learn oh so well.
So we grow up carrying this burden,
locked in our prison by fear,
with a secret that cannot be spoken,
intolerable to bear.

So how to break out of this prison?
Find the key to open the door?
How to get rid of the burden
and carry it no more?
For I did nothing, was not to blame,
yet I have carried the guilt,
sure I was bad and feeling ashamed
of the secret life I'd built.

And if the secrecy is sustained
how can I truly be free?
If I hide away as though ashamed
of all that happened to me,
it can only serve to perpetuate
the myth that I was to blame,
and strangely seems to invalidate
the meaning of my pain.

The pain of struggling to be free
from the chains of guilt and shame.

The pain of learning simply to be
just the person that I am.

There's only one way to find healing,
it is openly to share
to not be afraid of revealing
that secret innermost fear.

So this is why I don't want to use
a pseudonym, anonymous be.
And the reason why I freely choose
unashamedly to be me.
For never again can I collude
with fear, or the feelings of shame.
So at the risk of being misunderstood
I publish with my name.

And if it should be that anyone
insight or healing will gain,
then the cost to me of publishing
will not have been in vain."

Muriel, like many other survivors of childhood abuse, learned in the words of R. D. Laing that 'there is a great deal of pain in life and perhaps the only pain that can be avoided is the pain that comes from trying to avoid pain'. But this was to take her many years of struggle. For years, the defence mechanism of repressing childhood memories served her relatively well. It was the discovery that her silence had to be broken, her secret shared that enabled Muriel to discover a pathway leading to healing of the damage inflicted on her.

4

BREAKING SILENCE

Breaking the silence is vital for most survivors. They usually need to remember what happened and then to have as many opportunities as needed to share their stories. Such a pouring out and release of the feelings that go with it is an important factor in initiating healing. Survivors need to share their stories so that, falteringly, they can begin to trust people again after trust has been so badly betrayed. They also need to share as part of their search for freedom, understanding and acceptance. Some choose to go public about their stories, feeling they have nothing to hide and nothing about which to be ashamed. Their stories often encourage other people. Others are more private, are unable to go public on something so personal, and so they choose a very limited audience for their stories.

Such sharing or disclosure usually occurs in stages. These may, or may not, all be present and may or may not be in the order in which we mention them. Several stages may need to be repeated again at some point. Muriel identifies five stages in her disclosure:

INITIAL SHARING

Memories of what happened when she was little began to return in 1987 after nearly a year and a half of weekly psychotherapy. She remembers: "I'd just begun to trust John [her psychotherapist] but didn't know what to do with the memories that were suddenly returning to me. How could I possibly tell a man that I had been sexually abused? Was it all right to try? If I told him, would he want to go on working with me or might I risk losing him as a result? Perhaps he'd suggest I'd be better off with someone else – perhaps a woman therapist? My questions were endless and my fear was enormous. To be rejected by someone I'd just begun to trust (when trusting was so hard for me) seemed the worst thing that could happen to me.

"I was sick with fear about my first session with him after my memory of the abuse had begun to return. I knew deep inside that if I wanted to change and grow into being a more whole person, that eventually I would have to put him to the test and share it. So, I waited till a few minutes before the session was due to stop before raising the subject, so that I wouldn't have too long to confront the rejection I dreaded.

"I asked falteringly: 'Is there anything I can't talk about here?' He said something like, 'Do you really think there could be anything too terrible to bring to therapy? If you can't bring it here then where else could you take it?' There wasn't anywhere else. So, in a few trembling sentences I shared how I was beginning to remember the horror of having been sexually abused as a child. I explained what had triggered off the return of the memories.

"John listened with compassion, answered gently and with understanding saying that possibly this was the main (albeit unconscious) reason that I had begun to work in therapy. He explained that it would probably be the most important part of my life that we would need to examine and work at together. This was something he repeated many times in the succeeding years for I needed continual reassurance that it was all right to talk about this area of myself and that both he, and I and our relationship would survive it.

"I was vaguely conscious that he hadn't appeared surprised by what I shared. It almost seemed as if this was a missing piece of the mental jigsaw we were fitting together so painstakingly in therapy. I remembered his look of empathy and his gentleness and was slightly reassured. Perhaps it was going to be all right after all. For sure, there was no going back and we were now unable to escape the subject in future therapy sessions.

"I'd left sharing this till the end of the session and so my time was quickly gone. But then a new horror began when, out of the blue, I was overcome by a major panic attack –

the first ever to hit me. I was terrified. What had I done? During the week while I waited for my next session this panic and fear reached overwhelming proportions. Questions churned round in my mind. What did John really think of me and how would he respond to me in the future? Was it really all right to have shared this taboo subject with him? Part of me assumed that now that he had had time to assimilate what I had shared, he was sure to reject me. How could I ever look him in the face again without feeling overwhelmed by shame and wishing that the ground would open and swallow me up? How could he ever want to see me again? Inevitably he would now see me for what I felt myself to be – dirty and an object of shame.

"I began to wonder how ever I could manage to get to the next therapy session. I toyed with the idea of never returning but my need for help was greater than my fear. So on the day itself I dragged my feet from the station to his place, trying to delay the moment of arrival for as long as I could. I stood for ages outside his door mustering up the courage to ring the bell, longing to turn and hide, but there was no hiding place so I stood with my back to the door. Then the door opened, and there was John just as he always was, with his warm welcoming smile, and I lowered my head in shame.

"For months after that our sessions followed what I call a 'tell and run' pattern. The guilt and shame of admitting that I had been abused as a child so consumed me that I felt I could not survive the telling of my story. My constant assumption was that John would inevitably reject me and that seemed intolerable. Without realizing what was going on, I tried to handle this by first rejecting him. That way I could attempt to convince myself that he was no different from anyone else. This was happening at an unconscious level of my mind, and thankfully John noticed what was going on and refused to collude with it. Slowly but very surely my trust in him began to increase and I found I could share more and more."

WORDS FOR THE UNUTTERABLE

"At that time I had shared my story with just one other close friend, Sue. I had expected her attitude towards me to change or that she would end our friendship just as I had expected John to. But again my fears were not realized and Sue's unwavering support was vital in those early months, as I struggled with trying to overcome my overwhelming sense of shame and my terror that I would be rejected for what had happened to me as a child. Memories increasingly flooded me with horror and pain but thankfully not all at once. Like other people in a similar situation, I found that once this process of recall had started there was no way that I could stop it. It had a life of its own and continued to roll on at its own slow pace for about a year and a half. I constantly had fearful flashbacks into my past, often in nightmares and dreams, which usually preceded a more complete recall of any one particular experience. I continued to talk about all of this in therapy – thus beginning the second stage of disclosure, which involved finding words to explain a little more clearly just what it was that I was remembering and about which I was having nightmares.

"At this stage I said nothing about the precise details of what had taken place. I told myself firmly that I never could and never would talk about such a private and intimate matter. I even managed to convince myself that I wouldn't ever need to. John wisely didn't ask me for the details and didn't ever press or persuade me to share more than I felt able to at any one time. He could see I wasn't ready. Had he tried to get me to say more than I was ready to share, I might in some way have felt that he was abusing me – by misusing the power he had as my therapist to get me to do what he wanted, just as the baby-sitter had abused his power over me in the past. I suspect that I would have taken flight and perhaps never have had the courage to try to deal with the after-effects of abuse again.

"This stage of disclosure was agony. I couldn't bear the memories which flooded back unbidden and unwelcome. I never wanted to be the victim of sexual abuse. It wasn't supposed to happen in my kind of family – a 'nice Christian' church-going family. I began to see myself turning into an outcast with some kind of inner leprosy. I hated it all. Above all, I hated myself for being what I was and sat in my flat weeping with self-loathing for hours on end. In therapy I despaired because there was nothing I could do to make my abuse 'un-happen'. I tried to minimize it by saying that 'it wasn't as bad as incest', hoping that perhaps it would cease to plague me. But nothing changed my feelings about myself.

"Because of the secrecy, this stage of disclosure is also characterized by feelings of isolation and of being a freak. For this reason, with John's encouragement, I decided to try and find a support group for people like myself. This was easier said than done, for no one was able to tell me where to find such a group. I exhausted every avenue of help that I could think of. 'How can adult survivors of abuse find help?' I asked in each case. 'Are there any groups for us, adult survivors?' I always received a negative answer. My feelings of isolation were becoming so unbearable that it was increasingly vital for me to find other women who shared experiences similar to mine. I became desperate. About this time I had to go to the doctor for a routine visit. I sat down and he asked his standard question: 'How are you today?' As always, I replied, 'Fine!' But I was far from being fine – I was at breaking point. Something snapped inside me and I blurted out: 'Can we start this conversation again?' He looked surprised, but replied, 'Sure . . .'. And I then told him that I was far from being all right and burst into tears. He immediately put down his pen, moved his chair a little nearer and said: 'Off the record . . . no notes . . . what's wrong?' He was receptive, empathetic and listened intently while I told him my story of what had happened, of my terror and pain, of my sense of isolation and of my fear of disintegrating and falling apart. He assured me that I was not the first patient to share such a story in his surgery and gently asked me what I would like him to do to help. When I shared my pressing need to meet others like myself and my fruitless search, he replied: 'Leave it to me. I'll find you a group!' I did not expect him to be able, or to remember, to do this but true to his word he telephoned a couple of days later with a name and contact phone number for a group.

"My feelings were very mixed up by now. I was torn by

the tension of needing to be part of such a group and yet hated having to be associated with anything like this. Reluctantly I decided to give the group a try. Once there, I was overwhelmed by the number of other women in the room and by the realization that they were all survivors like me. Part of me tried desperately to convince myself that I didn't really need to be there, that I didn't belong in such a group, that I was not really one of them, and that I neither wanted nor needed to be part of them.

"To acknowledge that I was one with them, that I belonged there, meant that I was owning the unpalatable fact that I too was a damaged victim of abuse. I wanted to run away for I didn't like seeing myself in such a light. I was not ready to be so open about myself. Every fibre of my being screamed out the message that I had never asked for my memory to return as it had, that I preferred to remain in ignorance of my past, and that I did not want to have such hateful memories flooding back any more. I never asked to be the victim of sexual abuse and I felt resentful, trapped, helpless and powerless.

"I attended the group for two months before I opened my mouth. Previously I had sat on my own crying silently, unhappy and in total despair. Then to my surprise I realized one evening that I was unexpectedly ready to share my story with them, to explain what a misfit I felt, how I longed to deny reality, and how hard it was to accept that I too was one with them. I found myself saying: 'I am one of you – this is where I belong!' and it was an important pivotal point on my journey towards healing. However, it took many more years before I could begin to stop wishing that I could turn the clock backwards and live my childhood all over again, this time without the abuse.

"Now that I had talked about my story with my doctor and in the group, I found I had more courage to begin to talk about it with a few close friends. I was careful only to share with people with whom I felt safe and who I knew would accept me. People responded in different ways. Each person seemed shocked when I first spoke since they knew nothing about this part of my past. My relationship with some seemed little changed, with others a closer bond was formed – especially when, to my surprise, one or two friends revealed that they too were survivors. A few found my words hard to handle and seemed to withdraw from me. A few Christian friends could not resist giving me what they thought was good advice, telling me how I, as a Christian, should or should not be feeling, acting, speaking and thinking and how I should trust God and find healing from him. I knew in my heart that it was not as simple as that and that their way didn't seem to work for me."

ACCEPTING THE DAMAGE

"As time went on, I realized that the emotional damage I had suffered as a result of the abuse was far more extensive than I had first thought. My wounds were deep and were made worse by the silence and secrecy surrounding it all. It was at this point that I began to be in touch with some of the feelings I had carried through childhood and into other relationships and behaviour patterns as a result of the abuse.

"During this stage I came close to having a complete breakdown. My emotional pain was so severe that I thought I could not endure it through the blackest, most despairing months I had ever known. I still went to John weekly – dreading each session, yet unable to miss. I felt I could not contain my pain for the seven whole days between each session, and so we began to meet twice a week which eased things slightly.

"It seems to me that it was the therapy sessions which gave me enough nurture and sustenance to be able to carry on looking at my inner self and changing and growing. Professional counselling or psychotherapy is vital for many of us who have survived childhood abuse. Friends are important in our healing, and do all they can to help, but it is too much to expect them to provide that which is beyond their resources in terms of time, training, emotional and psychological experience. Some friends start off enthusiastically offering support, only to find that the feelings aroused by it swamp them and they have to withdraw. This can be worse than not offering help in the first place, for the survivor may then feel rejected yet again and the emotional damage will be further compounded. The most loving friends are those who are frank and able to explain their limitations but who offer love, concern and help in finding professional support if necessary."

DEALING WITH DISCLOSURE AND SECRECY

"What to say and when to say it was something that John left in my hands. He never probed into intimate details about what had been done to me but left it to me to tell him in my own time. I was grateful for this. In the depths of my confused distress I was dimly aware that before I could break out of my prison of secrecy, fear and shame, I was going to have to tell him what had taken place so that I could then walk tall and free again. Somehow I needed to find words and ways of explaining what my abuser had done to me but the memories churned round in my head finding an outlet only in recurrent bouts of nausea, vomiting and chronic feelings of illness.

"I couldn't face the agony of explaining what had happened. Most people feel shame, embarrassment or face other difficult feelings if asked simply to recount any 'normal' sexual experience. To share details of sexual abuse is excruciatingly painful in comparison. I found it even harder since my church and family background was one in which there was a conspiracy of silence when it came to talking about sex. Within this fundamentalistic religious culture there were unspoken rules like 'Don't talk about sex – it's taboo!' and 'Sex outside marriage is sinful!'

"But over the months, slowly and painfully, I began to share with John more precise details of my abuse. I often wished the floor would swallow me up, I was so embarrassed at times. I often found myself following my childhood pattern of communicating by the 'hint' method, expecting him magically to be able to thought-read and understand. I feared censure, repulsion or rejection as we talked but to my amazement received only acceptance and compassion. He seemed to care deeply about all I was going through and his gentle sensitivity encouraged me to go on sharing with him. It felt good to be affirmed so strongly, and his unconditional acceptance of me lifted the heavy cloak of fear I wore to hide the unacceptable human being that feared rejection if anyone saw underneath it to the real me. He knew, he saw and he accepted me, and this opened the way for some of my wounds to begin to heal. This nurturing enabled me to go on struggling to find freedom, to grow and to heal.

"But there was one particular aspect of having been abused which I dared not mention in therapy for many months for I felt too ashamed and guilty about it. I didn't know then that this aspect is a common facet of sexual abuse, but thought I was exceptionally 'bad' or 'sinful' because of it.

"Sexual abuse – especially in the beginning – usually involves touching and fondling which precedes genital stimulation. Such stimulation (no matter how unwilling or passive the victim may be) is sometimes followed by an orgasm. This is involuntary and as inevitable as the day follows the night. This means that for a few fleeting seconds a child may experience feelings of intense sexual pleasure which are not understood and which add to the confusion and distress which follow. This is one of the reasons why victims find it almost impossible to believe that they are not the one responsible for what happened. It seems to them that they must be guilty – for a tiny fragmented, split-off part of themselves involuntarily received pleasure in the middle of what was otherwise an unwanted and terrifying experience. When this is linked to masturbation learned through the abuse, then a cycle of guilt, fear, shame, blame and fear of rejection develops which may feel permanent or unchangeable. It was really hard for me to talk about all this in therapy (particularly because the subject was taboo in my church culture) but I knew that until I could bring it into the open I would remain imprisoned by the fears and fantasies inside my head.

"It was at this time that I discovered how to use my pain creatively in writing poetry. This helped to unlock the prison door and began to set me free. I poured out the details of my damage, distress and pain onto paper, I expressed my anger at my abuser, at God, at the Church, and at those who had failed to protect me from harm when I was little. The poetry helped John and me to examine the long-term damage the abuse had had on me, and it was poetry writing that led me to the final stage of breaking the chains of secrecy and the conspiracy of silence which had so damaged me."

BREAKING FREE

"I was wary about who I shared my story with until Sue read some of my poems and asked whether I had considered having them published. I was horrified by her suggestion. 'You don't have to put your name to it...' she explained. Her words gradually sunk in and I found myself grappling with questions like: 'Why go public? If I can't put my name to my writings, what am I saying? If I put my name to my writings then what will people think of me?' John and I explored the implications of these questions in therapy. Of what, I asked myself, was I ashamed? Something had been done to me, not by me. I wasn't too sure that others would see it this way though. One of the poems shared earlier in this book was born out of this exploration of becoming free from the chains of secrecy, guilt and shame.

"My willingness to go public has, however, been put to the test in a totally unexpected way. I was invited to take part in a BBC television Good Friday Service from Wells Cathedral – speaking about betrayal, the betrayal involved in abuse. I found I was able to do this – and to survive and grow from the experience.

"Healing the damage wrought by sexual abuse involves far more than mere acceptance of what happened in the dim and distant past. It involves integrating it into your whole life, making it part of the person you are now, and making it part of the person it is good for you to be."

5

GUILT AND SHAME

"I knew in my head that I wasn't to blame," Muriel recalls. "How could I have been? After all I was only eight years old when he started abusing me. But this intellectual knowledge didn't override my sense that inexplicably I must have done something to make it happen. Why else did he abuse me? Why pick on me? Surely I must have been giving out some kind of message indicating I was an easy target – and that was wrong of me. I'd been taught that adults were always right and knew best and that they weren't to be contradicted. So, part of me can understand how it was that I didn't really stand a chance and couldn't say 'No' to my abuser with his persuasive and frightening words – but another part of me blames myself for not finding a way of getting it stopped. As an adult I have a memory of being a child who knew deep down inside that what was happening was wrong and of being a child who didn't stop it. Guilt and shame consumed me for this."

Society in general may reinforce the confused guilty feelings of survivors. Typical of some is the Christian wife of an MP who on hearing how a young woman was used sexually by her church youth leader, stated: 'Obviously it was the girl's fault . . . it usually is . . . she could have prevented it but didn't. She's responsible for what happened.' Other often heard comments imply that little children may be so seductive and sexually provocative that grown adults cannot withstand their advances, or that children are likely to lie or exaggerate and are not to be believed when it comes to their word against the denial of an adult. Recent statements by leading members of the legal profession confirm this attitude is still prevalent. Such feelings abroad in society feed into the assumptions of survivors that they must be to blame and must be guilty in some way. The situation becomes still more confusing when the opposite is stated and survivors are also told that they are not to blame! Some even begin to feel guilty for feeling guilty.

Feelings of shame may make matters worse. For Muriel shame was one of the emotions of which she was first aware. She explains: "I'd received many messages about sex while I was growing up. There seemed to be something embarrassing and shameful about it. Religion reinforced this, adding that those who broke the rules would be punished by God or the Church. I knew someone who was actually excommunicated from the Church for their sexual behaviour, and began to believe that God wouldn't love me if I ever got that side of my life wrong. This made it even more important for me to keep my sexual relationships secret.

"I'm not sure how to explain the overwhelming shame that flooded me when memories of the abuse I'd suffered as a child began to surface in my memory. I wanted to disappear and never have to face anyone ever again. It seemed to me that if people found out about me they would be so horrified at what I'd done that they would disown me. It also felt as if my secret was out in the open and that my hidden shame was written in large letters all over me for all to read – as if others could not avoid seeing the glaringly obvious violation, dirt and degradation I tried so hard to conceal.

"I used to scrub myself hard in the bath, as if this would disinfect me inside. I felt like something displayed in a 'reject shop' or something bearing a notice 'shop soiled'. I was flawed, second-hand, spoiled and fit only for the rubbish tip. I was unclean, a social outcast to be shunned.

"I felt very bad for not having been able to tell the secret of my abuse. If I saw myself as bad then so must God, I reasoned, and so must everyone else. These feelings of guilt and blame left me so frightened and confused that when memories of the abuse returned I retired into my inner world, sharing myself only with my therapist."

Advice given to survivors can make matters worse. Guilt may be piled upon guilt if the person struggles valiantly but in vain to live up to the expectations of those whose confident words appear to be authoritative – as if their

utterances hold absolute truth for *everyone*. Such victims
absorb advice about how others think they *ought* to be react-
ing and acting but find that the standards set are impossible.
Yet again they feel that they 'fall short', unable to do what
is required of them – this time to forgive their abuser.

The sense that badness, guilt and wrongdoing ought to
be punished often hovers around. Muriel remembers how
she "was at a formal dinner party sitting near some members
of the legal profession when an enjoyable evening turned
into a nightmare. The subject of child sex abuse became a
topic of conversation following some newspaper articles
about it. People were saying things like 'Don't you think it's
all a bit overdone . . .', 'There's too much publicity these
days and it all gets blown up out of proportion . . .', 'You
know what kids are like . . . they exaggerate . . . they even
ask for it sometimes . . .' and 'What's wrong with a harmless
bit of fun . . .'. I could feel the colour draining out of my
face and felt sick and faint. It was as if I were on trial in one
of their courts. That night I dreamt that I was the prisoner
in the dock but that I had no defence lawyer to support my
cause nor was there a jury. I faced only the prosecuting
lawyer and the judge. I wrote about this dream:

> I wanted to tell, to shout and scream
> 'I was only a child m'lord,'
> but the defence of silence had been well learned,
> and I couldn't say a word.
> Silent and crushed by guilt and shame,
> defeated and sick at heart,
> filled with fear, alone and in pain
> I heard my sentence passed.
> It feels I've been punished twice over
> for a crime I didn't commit.
> Three years abuse of my body
> my innocence stolen by night.
> Forty years paying the on-going price
> denied what was mine by right.
>
> So many questions, they go round in my head
> until I can hardly think.
> Just one more – answer me this:

If I was not to blame, committed no crime
why was I punished at all?
I wrestle and struggle to understand,
my heart feels heavy and sad.
For the inescapable logic would seem
to be punished, I must have been bad.

"So the abuse began to seem like a punishment I had
brought on myself for being bad before it began. As I worked
on this in therapy I went through a stage in which my
increasing realization of just how badly the abuse had
affected me – so many different parts of my personality
damaged – left me feeling that all this pointed more and
more clearly to the extent of my badness. I was being punished by not being allowed things other people took for
granted and which I wanted – I was deprived of loving
committed intimate relationships, of healthy sexual relationships, husband, children and even of a family of my own
who would mourn for me when eventually I died. The punishment I thought God was meting out felt intolerable and
unbearable. I wrote:

> I'm ready to risk commitment
> to this kind of relationship.
> Such irony, such cruel fate,
> cruel punishment,
> for it feels that it's just too late.
>
> The silent tears run down my face
> they're plain for all to see,
> the naked pain, the feeling of waste
> that there's no one special for me.
>
> So what will the future be?
> I'm likely to die with no one to grieve
> or weep any tears for me.
> Stark reality."

For many survivors the feeling that punishment is deserved
can lead to self-punishing forms of behaviour. Some people
use alcohol, drugs or cigarettes, others abuse food, others
cut and burn themselves, others make suicide attempts or

find sexual partners who will hurt them. Muriel found she was punishing herself by doing something that seemed relatively innocuous. "I was a keen swimmer and used to swim a mile several times a week for fun. Returning memories of my abuse and the accompanying self-loathing and anger coincided with a Swimathon to raise money for a children's charity. I entered this and set myself an almost impossible target, forcing myself daily to increase the distance, and trying in this self-punishing schedule to work the anger out of my system – without success. I was exhausted by it."

The roots of feelings of guilt, shame, blame and punishment lie deep within us. As T. S. Eliot, in *The Elder Statesman* asks:

> What is this self inside us, the silent observer,
> Severe and speechless critic, who can
>   terrorize us.
> And urge us on to futile activity,
> And in the end, judge us still more severely
> For the error into which his own reproaches
>   drove us?

Many survivors of sexual abuse are harsh when it comes to looking at themselves. They judge themselves using critical and high standards, and quickly pronounce the verdict 'guilty', despite the fact that commonsense and rationality strive to assure them that they are unquestionably 'innocent'. Compassion for the child they once were, who was so hurt, tends to be conspicuous by its absence. What might have led to this state of affairs? How is it that some people are so merciless when it comes to judging themselves while accepting other people's humanity? How do such impossible (to someone looking from the outside) standards get set in the first place?

Sigmund Freud pioneered thinking about the complex processes involved in this. He suggests that after a child has fought a losing battle of wills with a powerful parent, the child's anger and possible destructive rage are not necessarily switched off. The child may appear complacent but, in Freud's words:

His own belligerent self... by preventing his escape from danger, will appear as the principle cause of his own suffering; so he will now feel towards himself the very hostility that . . . he previously felt towards the punishing parent, and condemn himself as he was first condemned by his parent. With whom, therefore, he may even come to feel he is in alliance against his own rebellious self. The child, being now divided against himself, is no longer striving against his parent; and, because it thus extricates the child from the external fight (the memory of which is eventually repressed) this process is likely to become habitual . . . [1]

Freud explains that this part of the child may then develop into an extremely strict conscience or, in his words, a 'punitive superego'.

Of course, such a child is not aware of what is happening in his inner world at an unconscious level when he lodges ('introjects') his parent's prohibiting force deep inside himself and it then becomes the voice of his conscience. The child simultaneously absorbs into himself positive aspects of his relationship with his parents and uses them as good models to copy. It is when these two different sides come into conflict that silent inner tension or obvious intense anxiety occurs. This may confuse the adult, who developed from that child, who is perplexed about his apparently inexplicable feelings or manages to blot out conscious awareness of them much or all of the time.

Thus some adults may feel guilty and sinful when commonsense and objective truth declare it impossible, and authoritative religious (parent-like) voices carry great weight and may feel overwhelmingly 'right' – and perhaps not even open to question. Such authorities are given the role formerly assumed by the inner parental voice and may become the voice of conscience.

Many people find their conscience is like a trustworthy, accepting friend who, when things go wrong, offers reassurance that next time things will be different and that basically all is well. But others are dogged by inner hints that they are inherently sinful, deserve to fail and inevitably must be 'guilty'.

Thus, a young adult may condemn herself because her father used her sexually when she was only four years old, and may see herself as a seducer. The conflict between her inner (often unconscious) urge to destroy her father versus her love for him and desire to protect him (both from himself and from herself) may threaten to overwhelm her at times.

For many survivors, it is not until they have understood and accepted the harshly judgemental part of themselves that they discover an inner ability to forgive themselves – even when, on the face of it, there is nothing for which forgiveness is really needed. Comments from others about 'ought's' and 'should's' may merely reinforce the voice of the hyper-critical conscience and superimpose more guilt on existing guilt.

This line of thinking was enlarged on by Carl Rogers who saw people as unhappy, self-destructive and anti-social, basically because they are unable to accept themselves as they really are. He blames this on social conditioning and on the kind of rearing which teaches a child that certain parts of it are unacceptable, dirty, shameful or bad, and that the child is a person of worth only when certain conditions are met, who can only be valued and loved by important adults when certain unacceptable aspects of self are denied. Eventually these externally imposed values become so much a part of the person that whole areas of experience have to be banished from any concept of self. At those moments when these banished parts refuse to remain quiescent and make their presence felt, the person concerned is likely to feel guilty.

Rogerian counselling and therapy offer a relationship of empathy, non-judgementalism and unconditional acceptance in the hope of changing long-imposed inner restrictions so that an individual can evaluate for him or herself rather than be compelled to follow values laid down by significant others. Change may occur, indicated by a moving away from outer facades, away from 'oughts', from meeting expectations, from a need to please others and instead towards self-direction, openness, to experience, acceptance of others and trust of self.

This, inevitably, like anything explained in such simple

terms, is less clear-cut than might appear at first glance. Freud and Rogers conflict with one another in areas that are important for the Christian. Freud believed that people needed the 'introjected constraints' of society's morality to prevent them from destroying each other. But Rogers saw those very constraints as the root cause of people's destructive aggressiveness. If this root could be dug out, he argued, then people's innate trustworthy impulses would be in harmony with the needs of others.

It is in this area that we run into two different streams of thought, each with different basic assumptions and, important for the thinking Christian, different streams of theological reasoning. Freud assumes each person at heart to be selfish and destructive and that any appearances to the contrary are not what they seem to be. Rogers, however, believes in each person's innate reasonableness and co-operativeness. From his point of view, any evidence of selfishness is the destructive result of our inhumane society.

This tension, obviously, becomes important for Christians in their struggle to connect feelings of guilt with a doctrine of sin. This is the more important because neither includes any direct thinking about God and God's relevance or irrelevance to the matter, or reflection on the theology of humanity.

The theologian John Macquarrie[2] explains that to Freud conscience was but one of the functions of the so-called 'superego'. Not only does it contain an understanding from childhood of what is acceptable and unacceptable behaviour but:

> We find Freud mentioning another phenomenon which has an obvious relation to conscience. This is the ego-ideal. This, we are told, is the vehicle 'by which the ego measures itself, towards which it strives, and whose demands for ever-increasing perfection it is always seeking to fulfil'.

So far, so good, but Macquarrie adds:

> The trouble is that Freud did not go far enough in developing the notion of the ego-ideal ... he had to account for everything in terms of the past. Thus ... he

deprives it of the possibility of any genuine creativity by effectively annexing it to the superego, so making the ego-ideal too a deposit from the past.

Macquarrie believes that Freud did not move far enough in the direction of a:

richer, more integrated conception of conscience [and that] he never actually reached it. The dynamism of conscience springs from the felt conflict, or at least, tension between those aspects of conscience which, in Freudian terminology, are designated the ego-ideal and the superego, the creative imaginative projecting of a moral goal and the static inheritance from the past. The first is concerned with creating value, the second with staying within guidelines. But Freud's account of the matter makes the tension or conflict impossible, because both the ego-ideal and the superego are referred back to the parents, and both are treated as deposits of the past. The basic error of this view is that it makes any advance in morality unintelligible. It would seem that advances in morality are most likely to occur when someone's personal ideals come into conflict with the generally accepted *mores* of society. But such a conflict is only possible if the personal ideal is in some respects independent of the *mores* and so morally transcendent. This implies that there must be a possibility of a creative projecting of ideals that have not wholly been inherited. Only so can something new be brought into the situation. But Freud's quasi-mechanistic view of the human mind appears to exclude this . . . but the indisputable fact is that they do break out.

This is highly relevant to some religious people who have been sexually abused. There are many emotional reasons why some have a tendency to feel inherently 'bad' or 'sinful' and therefore to feel an affinity with any stream of Christianity which is both authoritative and which caters for their need for 'sinfulness' to be forgiven, redeemed and sanctified.

The difference between Freud's and Rogers' view of humanity mirrors to some extent the tensions existing between the differing theological approaches of those who follow some form of traditional Augustinian theology (with its emphasis and basis on sin, original sin and redemption) and those who follow all or parts of the thinking related to Creation theology (with its emphasis on people's basic goodness, original blessing, and inter-connectedness).

Writing of Creation theology, Matthew Fox claims that:

> Original blessing is prior to any sin, original or less than original . . . maybe it was necessary for humanity to concentrate during a certain period on its fallenness. But the time has come to let anthropocentrism go, and with it let the preoccupation with human sinfulness give way to attention to divine grace. In this process sin itself will be more fully understood and more successfully dealt with.[3]

Choices eventually have to be made by individual Christians between the Augustinian teaching that 'the soul makes war with the body' and Creation spirituality which says in effect that 'the soul loves the body'. Such different paths cannot be traversed simultaneously. It is sometimes easy for someone who is the survivor of sexual abuse to slip into the former because it fits felt perceptions about the self, rather than for carefully thought-out theological or biblical reasons.

Carl Jung makes a striking observation about how people are and are not healed – something of relevance to the survivor of sexual abuse who longs for inner resolution. He writes:

> All the greatest and most important problems of life are fundamentally insoluble . . . They can never be solved, but are only outgrown. This 'outgrowing' proved on further investigation to require a new level of consciousness. Some higher or wider interest appeared on the patient's horizon, and through this broadening of his or her outlook the insoluble problem lost its urgency. It was not solved logically in its own terms but faded when confronted with a new and stronger life urge.[4]

6

COMING TO TERMS WITH THE PAST

'It's black and hopeless... I feel helpless... things will never get better inside me,' said Judy in shaky tones. To which another survivor replied with confidence: 'I've been forced to cling to the only thing I had – a thin thread called "hope"... and to hang on to it down the years... that's what's got me through when things were at their worst.' What had appeared to be only a cotton thread of hope turned out under testing to be made of unbreakable steel wire.

Sustaining Muriel, for a long time, was a flickering spark of hope that somehow it might be possible for her deep wounds to heal, that someone else might eventually turn up from somewhere who could understand and share her pain, that in the end she would be free from imprisonment in inner darkness and despair, and would one day experience a degree of wholeness and healing.

Such a healing process is sometimes referred to as 'coming to terms with the abuse'. On the face of it this may sound like a very Christian activity and a state it 'ought' to be relatively easy to attain. Some would reason that the past is the past, it is over and should be relegated to the past. However, the past is very present for all of us whether we realize it or not. Every survivor of sexual abuse carries scars and damage from the past into adult life and into patterns of relating and behaving.

We do not believe that 'coming to terms with the abuse' is about burying what happened and trying to forget about it. This, however, tends to be what families and friends expect of survivors and sometimes suggest in their well-meaning advice to, 'Leave it in the past where it belongs, don't rake it up again'. Yet the past itself often refuses to co-operate with such advice: once it begins to be recovered and memories start to return it has a habit of refusing to pretend it is dead, of refusing to lie down again and to stay comfortably and conveniently buried. 'When I started to remember what had happened,' shared one survivor:

> I wished I hadn't ever begun to recall things. I wanted to push everything back into my unconscious mind again – but it wouldn't go back, and more and more memories began to surface whether I wanted them to or not. This had a contradictory nature to it – for those unwanted memories had a welcome side to them for they shed light on things about my character that had puzzled me for ages. I also found that as memories surfaced and I managed to look long and hard at them, so healing commenced and I now see that those terrifying memories do not have the power to diminish or destroy me that I once feared they contained.

'Coming to terms with the abuse' also reaches deeper than mere acceptance of the past. Accepting and acknowledging that the abuse really did happen is vital, but more than this is the importance of realizing that both the abuse and the healing of some of its consequences are an integral part in the shaping of the survivor's character. Just as any other life-experience plays a part in shaping an individual, so too does the experience of being abused. One survivor explains:

> My abuse and its healing is a strategic part of all that makes me uniquely me, but I've had to work at making it an integral and valuable part. That's difficult. It's only recently that I've dared to explore the possibility that even this terrible experience could be precious for me . . . and I can see I need to explore this much more for I've touched on something really important.

We see 'coming to terms with the abuse' as being about journeying towards self-knowledge, self-worth, and seeking the freedom to love and be loved. It is a journey of change and growth, of emotional and spiritual healing and of becoming increasingly whole. Like every other worthwhile journey this one involves the expenditure of effort and energy – and is often expensive in cash terms. The destinations may seem unbelievably and despairingly far away and unreachable at times. Magic carpets are rarely provided (not even for the Christian survivor and not often in answer to prayer) but earthly sign-posts can be discovered, thick-soled shoes can be found and essential travelling companions are there once you know where to start looking for them.

Like all journeys this one has to have a starting place and a destination. The survivor often embarks on this journey when the story of abuse is really listened to and heard for the first time, is accepted in a non-judgemental manner and does not result in the giving of advice. A spark of hope is kindled and healing initiated when the story is accepted at face value, with warmth, is not trivialized, and scape-goating of the survivor (with subsequent apportioning of guilt and blame) is avoided.

Like many other vital journeys, this one is an immensely risky one to take. The risk of rejection can be paralysing. Unasked, unaskable questions may hover around like, 'Can I really trust you? Dare I expose my vulnerability, my pain and my nakedness to you? Will you use the knowledge I give you to harm me? When you see what I'm really like, will you be like the others and get rid of me somehow?'

The well-known psychiatrist specializing in marriage, Jack Dominian, explains the importance of being able to offer and to find the right quality of support. He writes that:

> Provided we have a sufficiently intimate and secure relationship with another person we can expose our wounds, which means we have to feel the pain of isolation, helplessness, worthlessness and rejection and communicate it. If the 'other' is sensitive enough to respond (and this is of course the risk we take, namely to explore our pain and be ignored or dismissed in the process, which simply magnifies the wound), then healing takes place. The 'other' can provide us with the ingredients of recognition, acceptance and appreciation which goes a long way to help us to unlearn our previous experience and substitute an appropriate one.[1]

Such a journey is usually impossible alone – a travelling companion is important. The 'successful' companion (as in job applications) 'will be someone' who is able to accept the traveller as he or she is when the journey commences (not as the companion might want them to become) and who is able to stick to the long and heavy commitment entailed.

Muriel recalls the pain she and her therapist 'companion' endured. "I didn't know anyone could experience such emotional pain and come out the other end without being destroyed by it but instinctively I knew that it was only by facing and going through all of this that my wounds could begin to heal. At times it seemed the nightmare would never end. Instead of getting better, it often felt worse after each session of therapy. I didn't understand it. Inside me was unbearable chaos. This felt like the opposite of the orderliness of healing. It felt as if a surgeon was relentlessly opening up, cutting away, ripping off and then re-opening raw infected wounds, was cauterizing, knifing and releasing pus, applying iodine to exposed jangling nerves, all without anaesthetic. I loathed it all but part of me sensed it had to be endured for healing to progress. To my surprise, each time a wound had to be re-opened in the intricate surgery of this stage of therapy, it was never again to become the open festering sore that it was when first we started working together.

"My inner chaos was made worse by a determination to appear outwardly composed and in control of myself at work and with most friends, regardless of the inner turmoil and suffering going on. I didn't want people to know what was happening to me. It was my secret. It belonged in therapy, but nowhere else. My pain felt intolerable and I'd beg my therapist to stop it somehow – as if he could! I longed to go to sleep and never wake up and irrationally feared I might be driven to end the pain by taking my life, or that it might destroy my mind and leave me mad. But at the same time there was a dim recognition that to give in would be to admit total defeat. This spurred me to fight back. I was reassured by words of Carl Jung's that I wasn't alone with my feelings and that someone like me might 'easily be overcome by a panic fear that he is slipping helplessly into some kind of madness he cannot understand . . .' And that:

So long as you feel human contact, the atmosphere of
mutual confidence, there is no danger; and even if you
have to face the terrors of insanity, or the shadowy
menace of suicide, there is still that area of human
faith, that certainty of understanding and of being
understood, no matter how black the night.[2]

"From time to time my therapist would confront me with
what was going on between us and I hated that. At times he
pointed out to me that it seemed as if I was playing games
to prevent us from facing difficult issues. At other times it
seemed that I was like the needle of a record player: stuck
in a groove and unable to move on. I hated being caught
out like this, and was inwardly furious with him for confronting me with issues I was trying to avoid. I rarely told him
how angry I really was for I was terrified he would abandon
me in retaliation. I could be furious about the abuse but
did not dare to be furious with John, but gradually I came
to learn that he was able to contain and hold all my angry
feelings without either of us being destroyed by them.

"Slowly, something important shifted inside me. I began
to recognize the value of my pain. It was like a warning
signal telling me that something was seriously wrong in my
inner world, that damage from my abuse was still demanding
and needing continued attention in therapy. Seeing the
value of the pain gave me the courage to cling to the jagged
edges of the precipices of this pain-filled part of my journey.
I also began to realize around this time that it was completely
unrealistic of me to expect, no matter how much I wanted
it, that healing, comfort and freedom from pain would be
total and forever! I could not expect my memory to be wiped
clean as if the abuse had never happened. Old scars could
be expected to flare up from time to time and, indeed,
often do gnaw painfully at me again, activated perhaps by a
comment, by something I have read or seen. When this
happens I can ask myself why, and know that it indicates I
have unfinished business with my abuse, that something
needs attention perhaps at a greater depth or from a different perspective. I suspect that it will be like this for the rest
of my life. Healing is occurring and will continue, I am
becoming increasingly whole and integrated, but I now

understand that it is all right for perfect wholeness not to occur in this life."

Few survivors are able to find the sort of help that initiates healing from family or friends – no matter how willing such close people may be. Practical expertise and professional training in working with survivors, possession of adequate emotional resources, support for the one involved in trying to help, time, and energy are rarely available from this source. This makes the option of seeking wise and supportive companionship for this particular journey from a professional counsellor or therapist important. Friends and relatives are not rendered redundant by this but are vital in offering extra support outside the counselling room.

Thinking about talking intimately to a stranger in a counselling situation may seem impossible at first to many people. A barrier goes up – it may seem that what is private (especially a family secret like sexual abuse) must stay private and cannot be discussed with anyone. The situation is made harder for those Christians who cannot accept the possibility that a Christian in emotional distress or suffering from a psychological problem could or should seek healing through secular counselling or psychotherapy. Fear may be expressed that faith will be undermined or totally destroyed. While respecting the integrity of those who genuinely feel like this, we would reiterate our personal experience that therapy has, for both of us, deepened our faith.

In some respects religion and psychotherapy share a common goal, as Carl Jung comments:

> What are we doing, we psychotherapists? We are trying to heal the suffering of the human mind, of the human psyche or human soul, and religions deal with the same problem. Therefore, our Lord himself is a healer; he is a doctor; he heals the sick and he deals with the troubles of the soul; that is exactly what we call Psychotherapy.[3]

Muriel shares: "Many people assumed I had lost my faith because at the time I started in psychotherapy I also stopped going to church – and didn't return to a church for four years. I needed freedom, time and space in which to reassess what meaning, if any, my lifelong allegiance to God and to the Church still had. What was I alive for? Was there any meaning or purpose to my life? It seemed as if my whole life had been spent trying my hardest to be what other people wanted or expected me to be. I was desperately weary from the effort of pretending to be what I was not, and was beginning to be able to be honest enough with myself to admit that inner reality and outer expression did not always correspond. I could see I needed to explore this disparity and try to understand what was going on.

"My first experience of seeking counselling help was perhaps easier for me than for some other Christians since it was my own vicar who put me in touch with Jenny, a professional counsellor, when I hit rock bottom and needed crisis counselling. I had his blessing on talking to her about the inconsolable pain of the loss of my career as a missionary. Those few months of working with Jenny were the beginning of a greater understanding of myself and the start of my journey towards wholeness, and left me convinced that this was something good that I needed to go on to explore. When I thought about more prolonged psychotherapy I began to hear Christian friends warning me that, 'It's self-indulgent introspection . . . you shouldn't spend time and money on yourself like that . . . you'll lose your faith . . .'. But I had to take the plunge – by then it seemed I had little left to lose and possibly much to gain. I doubted, I questioned, I was extremely uncomfortable, I feared my faith had disappeared and yet, through it all, I never lost the feeling that I had a spiritual part to me that made no sense unless God and my faith were genuine.

"Because my therapist was also a clergyman, I found it healing to be able to express and explore issues of faith that perplexed me. I thought of the possibility of never going to church again and that my faith might be meaningless. My concern about other peoples' opinions of me made this dangerous territory to explore. When they started asking me why I'd stopped going to church I was able to say I was having a sabbatical – that was fine for a year. By the time the year was up I felt more able to look people in the eye and say that I didn't know whether I'd ever be able to go to church again.

"I knew I couldn't carry on pretending to be someone or something I was not, nor pay lip-service to any belief system or creed that held no meaning or reality for me. My therapist helped my quest for ruthless honesty with myself by reminding me frequently that if God existed at all and was all he said he was, then my doubts, fears and questions were more than all right – they were welcomed by God! At times, to my perplexity, he would infer that my psychotherapeutic journey and my spiritual journey were one and the same thing and that at the centre of my being was God – waiting for me to find him there. With time I began to understand what he was talking about – I became increasingly aware of the wonder and mystery of God's presence within me, and my spiritual healing began."

Choice of the right therapist is obviously crucial in any psychotherapeutic relationship. Should one work with a male or with a female therapist? The answer is 'It all depends!' and even professional advice on the matter is divided. Some abused men and women are able to open fully and comfortably only with a woman. This is by no means a hard and fast rule, as Muriel found: "If I hadn't already been in therapy with a man before the abuse began to surface then I think I might have gone to a woman. It was a man who had abused me. How could I reveal this intensely private sexual material to a man? Could I trust this male therapist not to take advantage of my vulnerability nor to abuse me again in some kind of way? But the thought of starting with someone new was awful, and I had already begun to trust John enough to take the risk of staying with him and it turned out to be the best thing I could have done. It was a man who violated me and left me feeling dirty and degraded – it was now a man who played a vital part in giving me a relationship that was safe, non-abusive and healing."

Healing moments occur in therapy as Peter Rutter[4] explains, writing of professional relationships of trust in which one person assumes the role a parent would have had in the past – thereby making sexual activity forbidden, indeed almost incestuous. It is not unusual for clients to fall in love with therapists and thus to be very vulnerable – and the reverse may occur but less often:

When a forbidden-zone relationship becomes erotically

charged, several moments of decision inevitably occur that determine whether the sexuality will be contained psychologically or acted upon physically. Whenever a man relinquishes his sexual agenda towards his protégée in order to preserve her right to a non-sexual relationship, a healing moment occurs. Because so many women have been previously injured by the uncontained sexuality of men who have power over them, the potential healing power of restraint is enormous. Not only is the woman made safe from being exploited by this particular man, but the moment kindles the promise that she can be valued as a woman entirely apart from her sexual value to other men. In these moments, life takes a new turn, and injury from the past as well as hopelessness about the future can be healed. It may take many years for this moment to be realized ... for some women the healing moment was explicit, with the sexual possibilities of the forbidden-zone relationship discussed, acknowledged and relinquished. For other women the subject of sexuality never came up directly; the simple fact that the man never related sexually – at a time when the woman knew she was vulnerable to seduction – proved the healing moment.

Our experience of such 'forbidden-zone' relationships – those in which sexual acting out must be restrained because one person is in a position of power (teacher, therapist, clergy-person, doctor etc.) is that they extend also to same-sex sexual attraction, and to female power-holders as well as to male ones. It is as unethical for a woman therapist to touch and caress a woman client who loves her, to touch a male client who is sexually aroused by her, as it is for a male therapist to betray a female client sexually.

Muriel sums up her experience of the psychotherapeutic journey: "As far as I am concerned, the most important and best thing I have ever done is to invest time, money and energy in working in psychotherapy. Something like a conversion has occurred within me as therapy has transformed me from within, and it was the calibre of my therapist and the integrity of our relationship that made this possible.

He practised what the books taught were the essential components for good therapy, and became the one solid reliable rock on which I could depend despite my highly unstable inner world. His acceptance of me was a constant source of wonder and vital for my healing and something inside me began to change. Being what other people seemed to want me to be stopped being as important to me as it had in the past. I began to realize that I, too, was a valuable human being. It was good to be me! Self-worth, self-value and a measure of serenity and peace began to blossom from roots planted in therapy.

"I began to understand the meaning behind Jack Dominian's words:

> No freedom is as precious as that of fully possessing ourselves, having access to as much of ourselves as possible for it is from this ownership that the whole basis of being is safeguarded."

7

BURNING RAGE

Who was the person who stated dogmatically from the pulpit words to the effect that: 'Being nice is an important Christian virtue'?

We are unable to track him (or her) down. Tongue in cheek, we now suspect that no one has ever claimed this categorically in words of one syllable, and yet the consensus of unspoken opinion in some quarters seems to indicate that 'niceness' is a commodity indispensible to the life of every Christian. Some recognize the existence of this phenomenon and refer to it as 'the gospel of niceness'. Recipes suggested for producing masculine Christian 'niceness' rarely include a spoonful of anger and those for the feminine version always prohibit even a dash of anger-flavoured colouring. The result is the production of rather bland, innocuous – but very, very nice – people.

Angry women tend to be regarded as socially undesirable and to be avoided. Some Christians follow what we think of as the 'gentle Jesus meek and mild trend', and they and others may find and quote Bible verses like: 'Let all bitterness, and wrath, and anger ... be put away from you ...' (Ephesians 4:31) and 'Put to death therefore what is earthly in you . . . on account of these the wrath of God is coming . . . put them all away: anger, wrath ...' (Colossians 3:5–8). This may then be used to promote 'the gospel of niceness' to the exclusion of a more full-blooded form of Christianity. Gentle-Jesus-meek-and-mild trendies tend to avoid certain parts of the Bible. Passages ignored include, for example, those talking about the rightful place of appropriate anger (e.g. Eph. 4:26), or about the muscular Jesus who was so furious in the face of death at Lazarus's tomb that he snorted like an exasperated racehorse (John 11:33), or the Jesus who confronted evil-doing in the Temple by making a whip of cords and using it to drive traders out (John 2:15–17).

Muriel's uncovering of feelings of anger brought considerable confusion. It all began when her therapist gently suggested that it might be all right for her to feel angry about the abuse she had suffered. But Muriel recalls: "I heard what he said but it didn't feel all right. How could anger possibly be an appropriate response? I had been taught all my life that we Christians are supposed to be loving, kind and forgiving towards anyone who wants to hurt us. I understood this to be the way in which I could attain the desirable virtues of being 'victorious and triumphant' in the face of adversity. As a Christian, I knew I was not supposed to express angry feelings towards other people and certainly not towards God. As I understood it, the hallmark of true spirituality and of attaining every Christian's desired status of 'being in a right relationship with God' were to be found through practising self-denial, love and forgiveness. Qualities like these, I reckoned, were incompatible with angry feelings. My confusion was compounded though, since the therapist who told me that my anger was an appropriate response to my sexual abuse was wearing a clerical dog-collar and as such (by my reckoning) ought to be encouraging me to be 'nice' rather than inferring that being 'nasty and angry' might be acceptable in certain circumstances.

"At this time I knew next to nothing about the depth or extent of my anger – it was well concealed and well buried. Each time my therapist mentioned that it was possible that I might have felt angry about something I had talked about, I vehemently denied the possibility. Of course I didn't get angry, I reassured both myself and him. This state of affairs persisted throughout the early agonizing weeks of our sharing returning memories of my having been abused. It was much later on that I began to realize how greatly my childhood experience of abuse had corroded different aspects of my whole life, and it was then that I became aware of a profound sense of loss and deprivation. I realized that I had lost so much – including my innocence, my sense of self-worth and self-confidence, along with an ability easily to trust other people. I could see that it was hard for me to form stable relationships with men, and I lived with a gnawing low-grade fear that in the end I would be rejected and that the significant people in my life would abandon me and not be there for me when I needed their presence. By this time in my inner journey my Christian faith made little sense. It seemed as if much entrusted to me to be enjoyed as my birthright had been stolen from me by my abuser. It was at this stage in my life that I gradually realized the enormity of the hidden damage inflicted on me by him. And this was the point at which my pent-up anger began to seethe before finally boiling over; I felt like a volcano, threatening at any moment to erupt its larval contents and spew them out. I had no idea how to handle such strong and fearful feelings nor how to express them. I was terrified lest the eruption should take the form of a totally uncontrollable massive and dangerous explosion. Had my abuser still been alive and had I faced him at that stage in my life, I feel I could have killed him. But he was dead and I didn't know what to do with my mounting anger.

"So, I directed these feelings at God. After all, God was not physical or visible like another human being, and I felt safer venting my anger in this direction. This was made a little easier by the fact that I was now questioning my faith and it seemed to offer me a possible way of proving to myself that God was not really the loving, caring, protecting God I had been taught to accept as a child. I was very conscious that God had neither protected me from the abuse nor saved me from the painful and destructive after-effects it had on me. The God who had abandoned me did not seem to be connected with the loving and compassionate God beloved by my Sunday school teachers. My prayers turned into torrents of fury, in words like: 'Where were you when I was being abused? Why did you abandon me to the isolation of such a fate? Why didn't you intervene to stop it and to protect me? How is it that my perpetrator got away scot-free and I'm left carrying the blame?' I began to think that perhaps the time was coming for God and me to part ways. I was confused, fearful of the white-hot intensity of my rage and feeling increasingly helpless and hopeless.

"Therapy had taught me that feelings cannot be switched on and off to order – they do not respond like an electric light to the flick of a switch. I could not stop feeling angry.

I had also come to understand through therapy that feelings
are morally neutral things – they are neither right nor
wrong, neither good nor evil. They simply exist as do the
colours red and blue, the moon and the sun, the birds and
the fishes. They are a fact. But I struggled with teaching I had
received in the past about the place and value of feelings. I
had been taught that some feelings were acceptable and
others not, some were good and some were bad, and some
were right while others were wrong. My understanding of
the expectations the Church seemed to have about me and
about how important it was for me to be a 'nice' person
conflicted with some of the new understandings I was incorp-
orating into my life. My fear and my distress were further
increased when my anger was directed at God. How, I
wondered, could I possibly be as angry as this with God and
still be a Christian? It seemed then that nothing could ever
change the terrible destructive feelings I had for my abuser.
How, I asked myself, if perhaps God did exist could any God
possibly love me when I was as I was? Surely God would be
forced to withdraw his love and leave me as abandoned as I
had been as a child? This, in turn, exacerbated my anger.
Yet, strangely and inexplicably at this tumultuous time hope
was glimmering inside me – hope that there might be an
answer to my questions, that God just might still exist and
that if God was for real then that this God just might still
love me."

To feel angry is a natural part of being human although
these feelings are not always acceptable, recognized or
expressed. Anger tends to be misunderstood, can seem confusing and very powerful. For this reason it is one of the
human emotions most feared, especially since *feeling* angry
may well be confused with *expressing* anger. This inability to
distinguish between angry feelings and angry actions sometimes leads us to conclude that anger in any form is 'bad'
and to be despised, rejected or overcome. Our fear may be
that our anger will get out of control and lead us to harm
ourselves or someone else.

What then can we do with our anger? Since feelings are
feelings and as such are neither right nor wrong, good nor
bad, they cannot bring about damage unless they are acted
on. Feelings in themselves are neutral. However, they must

be brought into the open as far as possible and their existence acknowledged if they are to remain harmless. This
opens up the possibility of exploring the angry feelings that
threaten to tear us and others apart in their destructiveness,
and perhaps discovering that they are a healthy response to
pain – and especially to the violation of abuse. As such,
angry feelings play an important part in bringing about
healing and transformation and can thus be welcome. Being
in contact with the powerful force of our anger gives us the
option of choosing how to use it – whether to express it in
some way and to act on it and, if this option is taken up, of
finding a safe and appropriate way of doing so.

Many Christians find it harder to own their angry feelings
than do other people. Following the 'gospel of niceness'
philosophy leads many Christian groups to evade and deny
the existence of anger – either in group members or in the
group as a whole – and therefore the anger is driven underground and any bottled-up anger is exacerbated. Christians
neither like being around their angry selves nor an angry
God, and so like children seeing ghosts in bedtime shadows,
they fear that which they only half understand, which lurks
in the unseen shadows and grows bigger in the darkness.

Alastair Campbell[1] suggests that:

> Faced with injustice, the contempt of others, the affront
> of death or just the petty frustrations of living with
> others, those who fear and deny anger experience a
> gnawing guilt which drives them deeper into themselves
> and further away from the true causes of their anger.

He quotes[2] a Report on the psychological problems in the
Church of Scotland by H. A. Eadie, who concludes that
anger is an even greater problem for the modern clergyman
than unacceptable sexual fantasies. He quotes from the
Report, saying that:

> Aggressive impulses stimulate even greater anxiety and
> guilt in the clergyman. Any anger, hostility, or even
> competitive self-assertion, in himself or others, must be
> rigorously controlled and, if possible, rejected. These
> impulses, which are apparently in conflict with 'Christ-
> ian' values of self-denial and non-aggression, are

rejected by striving to attain the ideal of being a loving person.

This leaves Christians grappling – consciously or more often unconsciously – with the two apparently irreconcilable opposites of love and anger. The one appears to be unable to survive in the presence of the other. It seems impossible that the two can be balanced and held in tension in the same person at the same time. We fear that anger will destroy love, and that anger within a relationship will at best merely dent the relationship but at worst will totally destroy it. We carry such feelings into our thinking about God.

However, we would contend that these apparently irreconcilable opposites are not mutually exclusive and can be held together within their tensions. Such opposing polarities of feeling can be woven together into a web with the strands that emanate from them.

Muriel is not alone in experiencing the damage caused by all forms of sexual abuse and the buried anger associated with it. In 1982, Anna Freud went on record as ranking incest higher than any other form of abuse in its potential for causing emotional damage and harming a child's normal emotional development. In 1988, Johanek noted that there may be an 'arrest of emotional and social development, which began around the time of the original assault'. The roots of anger may be buried in this earth and reveal themselves in different ways in different people. Little children have to find their own unconscious emotional mechanisms for coping with the inadmissable reality that the parents (or trusted adults) on which they should have been able to depend for care and protection have been the ones to betray them by giving the opposite in life.

Some, as we have seen, will attempt to cope by shifting responsibility for what happened away from the adults and back onto themselves – they assume the blame, feeling that they were seductive enough or bad enough to have caused the abuse. It is easier for small children to do this than to face the impossible admission that in reality an important care-giver really loved them so little that they were treated very badly. Some children then find that without thinking about it deeply, they assume that it was their own innate evil which led to the abuse or to other family members ignoring what was happening at home. This unconscious assumption may also be less painful than having to confront the fearful reality (for a child) that one is totally powerless and that such happenings are completely beyond one's control. Without knowing that this is happening, or thinking about it logically or reasonably, children easily assume omnipotence – a great sense of power – and can readily feel that *they* have *made* the *adult* abuse them.

Another way in which children cope is by regarding adult male relatives as being too weak to be able to stand up to what is felt to be 'seduction' by the child. This enables the child to regain its vital need to feel it has control over events in its life. Thus, children who have been sexually abused tend to be quick in learning how to deny or repress their unbearably bad feelings about what is happening to them, and are then unable to connect with any feelings about it all.

This may appear to work successfully for children but when this coping mechanism is carried into the unconscious motivations of adult life (as it very often is) it may have the important consequence of the person being handicapped through being unable to express anger at the abuser and others involved. The anger may be felt (even if the feeling is unconscious and therefore unrecognized at a conscious level of the mind) to contain the potential for devastating, overwhelming violence and unknown danger, and therefore it must be held in tight rein for once released there may be a sense that not only will the perpetrator be destroyed but also the survivor her/himself. These feelings are rarely understood outside counselling or therapy and usually remain buried. Such anger may then be directed inwards, being transformed into self-hatred and often leading to self-destructive behaviour.

Some children find another way of handling the unhandle-able by minimizing the importance of what happened to them. This is not a carefully thought out way of handling things but is an inherent coping mechanism and the person concerned rarely realizes they are employing it. Instead of being in touch with terrifying angry feelings they may try rationalizing them with reassuring and anaesthetizing thoughts, such as: 'It's really not too bad ... it'll soon be over', 'It's just part of growing up and doesn't matter too much', 'I can't do much about it so I'll just stay with it till it's over and then ignore it', 'This isn't happening to *me* – I'll just take myself away in imagination till it's over – and then it won't really have happened to me'.

Others use teaching about right and wrong to try to make sense of their abuse. Feelings may run along these lines: 'What Daddy says is always right. Therefore, if he says we have a little secret between us then that is all right', 'Daddy says that Mummy will get upset if she finds out our secret. If she finds out and gets upset then her getting upset will be my fault for being bad, and so she mustn't ever get to know', 'If Mummy gets upset then she'll be hurt and that might destroy her and I'd have done something really bad', 'As I'm ten years old and this happened to the others when they were ten it's all right – it's just part of growing up – and so it's not bad'.

Many children have mentally to revise their expectation that adult care-givers can be expected to care for them, jumping through hoops in the contortions of mental gymnastics. Their thinking may run along these lines: 'He shouldn't do that to me ... but I know he's a man and men can't be trusted ... that's how it came about in the first place ... and Mummy knew he was doing it and didn't stop him ... so that means that she can't be trusted either. That leaves no one on whom I can rely except myself – so I've got to get on on my own and that's got to be all right.'

This was an understanding, a slowly growing empathy and compassion which eventually turned to forgiveness, which Maggie found at the time of her father's death.

> They rang in the dark to say he'd died
> Driving down the next day to my mother's
> a foul litany emerges on the North Circular Road.
> Pederast
> Mother-Fucker
> Child molester
> Malefactor

Pederast – which he wasn't really
Mother-Fucker – which he wasn't either
Child molester – which he was
Malefactor – which we all are . . .

Pederast
Mother-Fucker
Child molester
Malefactor
and the Lord turned
to the malefactor on his left
and said,
'This day shalt thou be with me in Paradise.'
Pederastmotherfuckerchildmolestermalefactor
what if someone shouts it out at the funeral?
close the lips I can,
edit the unfamiliar words
and shut off the mind I cannot.

For Maggie, finding healing and the ability to forgive necessitated her being willing to forgo the luxury of following the comfortable 'gospel of niceness' and plunging into the murk of exploring the depths of her fury. Exploring that which is buried is a risky business – who knows whether it will turn out to be a landmine or a crock of gold?

8

HEAL WITH ANGER

Far from being something that is 'bad, sinful or evil' to be got rid of as swiftly and efficiently as possible, anger has rightly been called 'the backbone to healing' and can not only be both a healthy response to violation but also a powerful transforming energy. Instead of burning with anger survivors can heal with anger.

But before this can take place most people have to work hard at understanding what anger has done in their own lives and the way in which it gets ignored, is unacknowledged or unexpressed, and the potential it has for causing serious insidious damage. Our minds can play tricks on us and lead us to deal with unacceptable and unwanted feelings in different underground ways – and these may sabotage our total personalities and undermine what we attempt to live up to and the people we try to be.

Sometimes, without knowing this is happening to us, we employ the defence mechanism known as 'repression'. This involves us in, unknowingly, banishing painful impulses, desires or fears from our conscious minds and secreting them away in the hidden recesses of our deepest selves so that we ourselves are unaware of their presence. Another common, similar defence mechanism is called 'suppression' and occurs when we consciously exclude painful thoughts or desires from our awareness. Both these techniques – one completely unconscious and the other more conscious – have the same end result. Buried anger is 'out of sight' and thus optimistically, we might reckon, 'out of mind'. However, this anger is far from being dead; it is like something that has been buried alive in our minds which may make its presence felt, playing havoc with our deepest feelings.

Buried anger has a devastating effect for, turned inwards,

it has an insidious poisoning effect on us. Adrienne Rich suggests that 'most women have not even been able to touch this anger, except to drive it inward like a rusty nail'.[1] In some people buried anger is the root cause of depression. For others, it leads to illnesses which show themselves in the body. Some joint, skin and intestinal problems are rooted in anger which has been buried and are therefore not cured by medicines but only treated adequately when the causative anger has surfaced and been dealt with appropriately.

Other people deal with their anger by unconsciously depositing it in a person, a situation or a place other than the one where it truly belongs or by scattering it at random all over the place. Putting it where it really belongs seems too risky. The problem for most of us is that this is done by a buried and hidden part of the mind without the conscious, rational, intellectual part being consulted first. Typically this mechanism is at work when someone comes home from work furious with the boss and is then angry with his or her partner instead of with the boss. With hindsight, some survivors have realized that their anger with their abuser has been vented in later life on their own children – but they did not realize that they were doing this.

As someone explained:

> One of the first clues I get which alerts me to the fact that something is wrong at a level of myself that I'm rarely in touch with is when I realize that I'm getting irritable with virtually anyone who crosses my path . . . really fed-up with them about stupid minor things. These over-the-top feelings of annoyance can be used as useful warning signs to me that something is going on at a deep level of myself . . . I find it's worth my while trying to understand what may be happening inside myself and then trying to sort it out. Often it turns out to be linked with my anger or fear at my past abuse.

Anger that is displaced may find its outlet in verbal or other ways. Should it turn to violence then it is wise to seek professional help for violence cannot creatively be met with further physical violence. This is destructive to all concerned.

Anger may sometimes be stifled by being stuffed with

food, drowned in drink or anaesthetized with other drugs. At other times, it may be expressed through self-destructive or self-punishing behaviour: eating disorders, drinking heavily, drug-taking or through hurting oneself. During a course of therapy, Sarah became aware that she often went through times when she, in her own words, 'looked like a grown-up battered baby'. At these times her body would be covered with bruises which she realized she must have inflicted on herself by walking carelessly and banging into furniture, doors and walls and tripping over without fully realizing what was happening. When she began to explore how she managed to hurt herself and what it might be indicating, she began to understand that this happened to her at times when she was burying guilty feelings for having (as she felt) been a 'seductive toddler' and having – she felt – induced her uncle to make love to her. She was unconsciously giving herself the punishment she felt she deserved for being so bad. Obviously this was not rational behaviour, for she was not aware of her need to punish herself.

Eating disorders and self-mutilation are ways in which some people act out their enormous rage against themselves – against the self which they feel at an unconscious level of themselves to be responsible and to blame for their abuse having taken place. There may be an element in this, for some people, of making sure that their bodies will no longer be attractive to men.

The ultimate self-destructive act is suicide and for some people this seems to be the only way of escape from intolerable inner agony. It is also a powerful statement of the total despair felt by many. Jane explains:

> I've never tried to kill myself but I have often felt like ending it all. Several years ago, when I was first remembering the abuse, I was terrified of all the feelings surfacing in myself and longed to go to sleep and never to wake up again. If only I could find some kind of anaesthetic ... something permanent like death ... it would have brought relief from what was becoming intolerable. At times, feeling abandoned and isolated has increased my overwhelming sense of despair and of pain, and in the darkness of the night I've found

thoughts and plans revolving in my mind as to how I might put a permanent end to it all. On a couple of occasions this urge was very powerful and I hate remembering those times. There seemed to be nothing worthwhile in me, I despaired of everything, and underneath all of this there was a feeling of intense murderous rage . . .

Such deep feelings which direct anger against the self are closely linked to a sense of having been responsible for the abuse, of being to blame and of being guilty.

Muriel remembers a stage in which guilt and blame consumed her. "I was sure that it was all my fault. I felt that I must have been provocative and seductive to make him desire and use me so often sexually. Further, I had let it happen and hadn't stopped it. I told myself often that I didn't say 'No'. What was worse, my body used to respond sexually to his arousal and that felt terrible to me. How could I have been that bad. When I wept about this to my therapist he would gently respond with words like: 'But you were only an eight-year-old child – you didn't have the power to say "No".' His words added to my distress. I hated the fact that I had been so powerless. I hated my body. I hated every part of me. My anger and my hatred were so mixed up together that it wasn't until I began to be able to love and to value the person that I am that I began to lose some of my self-hatred and to see that the responsibility, blame and guilt belong elsewhere and not with me – they belong with my abuser. Having reached this point, I then found that my anger could be expressed in ways more appropriate than berating and punishing myself."

Anger may need to be targeted in a particular direction. For survivors of abuse, anger often needs to be redirected at the perpetrator. Muriel remembers that she was very angry with her abuser "but it was a long time before I could deal with my feelings about him – I was far too frightened to do so. This meant that for a long time I thought about the things he'd done to me and the damage he had caused. Like any little child I had longed for love and affection – instead of this he had given me sexual stimulation and arousal. At eight years old I had lost my innocence and

carried the wounds of this damage into my adult sexual
being. My trust in the world of adults was shattered and I
still find it hard to trust others, especially men. Irrationally
I am still afraid of being abandoned by those people who
are important to me and deep down inside myself I know
that I don't really expect them to be there for me when I
am in need or in pain. I feel that they are bound to go away
just when I most need them. Every part of my life seems to
be affected by my childhood experiences. I knew I had
plenty about which to be angry but it was a long time before
I was able to concentrate on thinking of my abuser himself
rather than of the abuse. But when I did it seemed to me
to be much more to do with the abuse of power than anything else. My abuser had exerted his adult power over me
leaving me powerless and helpless. And this was all so subtle
that I accepted the responsibility for all that he did to
me! Realizing this facet of what had happened infuriated me.
How dare he walk away and leave me with my feelings of
guilt, shame and the sense that I was somehow to blame for
what he had done to me. For a long time his power over
me was such that I still found it difficult to talk about him
even in therapy – almost as if talking about him would free
him to exert his power over me again and reach out from
his grave to damage me. Eventually I was able to vent my
feelings in this poem:

> To think all these years I've carried
> your guilt and blame as mine.
> Thinking somehow it was me who was bad,
> although you committed the crime.
> Such was the power you had.
> What you did was a crime
> you were guilty!
> This guilt was never mine
> it makes me feel so angry
> that I've carried it all this time.
> I doubt that I will ever forget
> the anger and pain you have caused.
> But the feelings of shame,
> the guilt and the blame
> I disown, for they are yours."

Muriel adds that "penning these words was liberating and freeing for me."

But perhaps the most significant moments of healing came for Muriel in two separate but consecutive Communion services. It was with new insight that she understood that when Jesus used the little child he sat on his knee to teach the disciples about the important qualities of simple, humble trust, love and obedience, he also gave a glimpse of the fierce anger he feels towards anyone who harms a child in any way (Mark 10:13).

As Muriel reflected on this she comments: "This was the first glimpse I had of the possibility that Christ shared my anger about my abuse. The abused little child I once was and now carry within me, was one of those children about whom Jesus spoke with such tenderness and such protective anger. It began to seem possible that I could loosen my grip on my desire for revenge and my wish to see my abuser properly punished for what he had done to me; leave it to God to see that justice was done. This was a liberating and healing moment for me."

The story of how Jesus cleansed the Temple became a story of further hope. Muriel comments: "Here was Jesus at his most angry, and his anger was because the Temple of God had been desecrated (John 2:15–21). Later, thinking about the biblical teaching about our bodies being the temple of the Holy Spirit, I remembered the Bible verse that says: 'Do you not know that you are God's temple and that God's Spirit dwells in you? If anyone destroys God's temple, God will destroy him. For God's temple is holy and that temple you are' (1 Cor. 3:16–17). I read these verses with a dawning sense of wonder and awe. It was awesome realizing that this body of mine, which had been sexually violated when I was a child, is a temple of the living God. I sensed that not only was it right for me to be angry at what had happened to my body but that Christ too shared my anger at the rape of this sacred, innermost part of myself. My feelings at that moment were ones of overwhelming wonder that my broken and flawed humanity was a temple in which the holy and awesome God has chosen to dwell.

"As was my custom, I talked this through with my Spiritual Director and he shared thoughts of his which built on mine.

He asked a couple of searching questions about what it was that the money-changers had actually done, and what exactly had happened in the Temple after Jesus had thrown them out. I could see that the money-changers had stolen money and exploited vulnerable people but I had not seen before that they had also robbed ordinary people of their rightful use of the Temple. The place which should have been a place of prayer and healing was used for that purpose, as Matthew records (Matt. 21:14), only after Jesus had expressed his anger and righted the wrong: 'And the blind and the lame came to him in the Temple, and he healed them.' This was important to me and reinforced my own feelings that despite the depths of my despair and fury at times, God is present not as a disinterested observer but rather as one who shares my anger and pain and as one in whom resides an added potential for healing. This offers me hope that Christ's healing power will be active to help transform my damaged self through his life and love. I have thus found a close link between my anger and God's unconditional and healing love. As I write this I am aware that this is something I lose sight of all too quickly and need to hang on to continually lest my own lack of self-worth, my own anger and hatred turn inwards and lead me, yet again, to assume that it is impossible for anyone, let alone God, to love me."

Another area where anger may begin to surface for the survivor is related to feelings about parents. This can be confusing, especially for someone who has grown up in a religious atmosphere in which emphasis is placed on honouring parents and on teachings that, like oil and water, anger and love cannot possibly be mixed or even co-exist side by side.

One survivor shares:

> I couldn't be angry with my mother for ages. I love her dearly and was afraid that if I was really in touch with my deep disquieting feelings about her that these might destroy my love for her. It wasn't so difficult with Dad. I was angry that it was he who had introduced my abuser to our family and trusted him with me. But my real anger is that I tried to tell my parents what was going

on when I was alone with the man and they didn't seem to understand the hints I was dropping or to be able to read between the lines. I couldn't tell them plainly what was happening to me because my abuser threatened to hurt me should they find out... but I was sure my parents could see how much I hated being left with the man and they didn't do anything about it.

Feelings about women in general and about mothers in particular can be complex. In our society it is often women (and very often mothers) who tend, often unjustly, to find themselves the targets of anger. They may find themselves scapegoated for things that are not their direct responsibility – like a father's sexual use of his children. This may come from different directions in the family. The father may some-times try to justify his actions with words like: 'It's all my wife's fault . . . she doesn't give me enough of the right kind of sex . . . she doesn't really love me as I need to be loved. . .' He may add that she has a drink problem, that she's always tired or unwell, or is not available for him when she's feeding a baby or on night-duty at work. He may then plead in words more fitting (we think) to a helpless child than an adult man: 'What was I expected to do . . . things were desperate and I couldn't help myself . . . I can't live without enough sex and without really satisfying sex . . . I was forced to turn to my daughter instead of my wife because she was the only person available to meet my needs . . .'

Our feelings are often mixed about our mothers and other people's mothers. Deep inside ourselves we carry timeless pictures, vividly expressed in art and literature, of one type of mother who is really good, loving and nurturing and another who is bad, destructive and devouring. Most of us finally manage to find a compromise in our minds between these two extremes when it comes to picturing our own mothers – although some of us veer more towards one extreme than the other.

While mothers may be negligent, deliberately harmful or bury their heads in the sand when it comes to protecting their children from abuse, we are concerned about the times when they are blamed too much for the actions of others and especially fathers – as if they are responsible for controlling their partner's sexual activity and can be called to account for his actions. Yet, paradoxically, our concern is muted by our realization that a part of us does blame the mother for not doing just this – after all, we feel, this is what mothers are for! We thus collude with society's attitudes towards women at those times when we allow this kind of feeling to go unchecked. It may be more comfortable for us to blame a woman than to blame a man. So, we point an accusing finger at the mother who was the 'silent partner' through her knowledge (real or supposed, conscious or unconscious) and failure to intervene to protect her child.

Obviously there are many survivors who blame their mothers and feel angry, with justification. The mother may have been the abuser herself or she may have set the son or daughter up to be to her husband what she could or would not be. She may have known what was happening and failed to intervene out of fear or indifference, or even out of a misplaced religious conviction that, since she believes that the husband is supposed to be the 'head' of his wife and his family, he owns them and has a right to do with them what he will – and this may include inappropriate sexual activity with a child. Such a wife may find that she is torn between her religious convictions and her heart, or that she uses her religion to bolster her unwillingness or inability to intervene for other reasons.

Feelings about parents can be very difficult to unscramble. How, some survivors wonder, can it be all right to feel angry with your parents when as a Christian you are supposed to obey the teaching in the Bible to 'honour and obey' them? How can you both love and hate somebody and how can you possibly hate someone whom you love very much indeed? The confusion is compounded when the abuser is a loved member of the family: a father, a mother, a grandparent or a sibling.

Some survivors are told in church situations that everything will be all right for them if only they learn to love their abuser, but it doesn't seem to work out as simply and naively as some of those giving out this advice assume will be the case. The survivor is merely left with an additional weight of guilt at not being able to manufacture loving feelings to order, and may feel increasingly isolated and alienated. The myth that the survivor is in the wrong and is a bad person is strengthened. It is healing when – as happens all too rarely – it is possible for family members to listen to the survivor's feelings, to stay with the awfulness of the experience shared, and to talk and accept these painful feelings within the family circle. Blessed is the family that can accept feelings for what they are, without running away from the pain of them and dishing out excuses, blame or scapegoating, or trying to make everything better so quickly that the seriousness of the feelings seems to be rubbished.

Christian survivors often have a problem with their church. As we saw in Chapter 3, unhelpful rejecting comments abound. One church leader, publically and in the hearing of two Christian survivors from his church, declared that his church couldn't possibly contain anything as 'bad' as survivors of sexual abuse – as if such people were contaminated with a kind of leprosy and his church was too nice for 'that'. We know of another churchman who is quoted as stating: 'What's all the fuss about? In the past when a mother died it was natural for the father to have sex with a daughter instead of his wife. So why can't it be accepted as a normal part of family life nowadays?'

As well as feeling angry with the abuser and with the family, many Christian survivors feel angry with their church and with society in general for apparently failing to take the subject of sexual abuse seriously enough. Despite media attention and greater awareness of sexual abuse, it seems to many that the subject is hived off onto a side-road where it can be passed easily by. Survivors may feel they are some kind of 'export reject', to be off-loaded on a jumble sale and given second-rate treatment. Few church pastoral teams have team members trained in working with survivors in the church. Even fewer churches have or make funds available to help survivors get professional counselling or help through therapy. It is left to the survivor to foot the bill and to pay for the help that may heal the wounds of abuse. To some people this seems like another form of injustice but others recognize that is good for survivors to value themselves enough to pay for their own treatment and healing. However, healing often involves long and expensive treatment and finances are often the only barrier stopping a survivor from seeking the much needed help.

There are, however, ways in which anger can be expressed positively. Ellen Bass and Laura Davis[2] make some helpful suggestions. They write:

> Whether you express your anger directly to the abuser or you work with it yourself, it's essential that you give it some outlet. You can speak out; write letters (either to send or purely for the chance to get your feelings out); pound on the bed with a tennis racquet; break old dishes; scream (get a friend to scream with you); create an anger ritual (burn an effigy on the beach); take a course in martial arts; visualize punching and kicking the abuser when you do aerobics; organize a survivors' march; volunteer at a recycling centre and smash glass; dance an anger dance. The list is endless. You can be creative with your anger. And ultimately you can heal with anger.

In the words of Barbara Deming:[3]

> Our task of course is to transmute the anger that is affliction into the anger that is determination to bring about change. I think in fact that one could give that as a definition of revolution.

9

COSTING FORGIVENESS

Fran clenched her lips, wanting to scream out in protest, but instead fixed her lips in the frozen smile mastered in childhood. She turned to the earnest, very 'Christian' woman on her left and listened passively to words she had heard repeatedly in the past – like the needle of a record player stuck in a groove.

The woman came out with a well-worn formula, guaranteed by certain of her church leaders to turn Fran (or anyone else deemed to be 'straying from God's pathway') into 'successful', 'triumphant' or 'victorious' Christians. Her words oozed out:

> You've only got to forgive him and then everything will be all right. You can't continue being so angry. Just forgive your abuser, bring him to God's mercy seat in prayer, and you'll be transformed. Remember, my dear, God is only going to forgive you to the extent that you forgive others – after all, Jesus taught us this in the Lord's Prayer, didn't he?

Fran's shoulders tensed, she gazed blank-eyed, empty-hearted at the woman – would no one ever understand that forgiveness didn't appear to order? Could this woman even begin to understand how it was to be Fran? In those rare moments when she could be ruthlessly honest with herself, Fran realized that she didn't just dislike her abuser – she hated him with cold, bitter, knife-twisting feelings. She was more than 'angry' with him, and earlier attempts at forgiving him had left her more confused, desperate and guilty than ever. She sensed she was destined to fail. Forgiveness was a commodity that she could not dredge up from within herself, and neither mail-order catalogues nor God sent it to her to order. She could not make the past 'un-happen' by trying to ignore its existence.

Thoughts about the possibility – and impossibility – of trying to forgive one's abuser are often inescapable for many survivors (whether Christian or not) once they have taken steps along a path heading in the direction of healing. For many Christians this subject causes particular additional stress and heartache. Books tend to come up with two general answers suggesting:

- either that forgiving the perpetrator is not really necessary – it is forgiving oneself that is really important;
- or that Christians *must* forgive their abusers – for this is seen to be an indispensible prerequisite to receiving God's forgiveness. They argue that you cannot have one without the other. Unless you forgive your abuser, God *cannot* (it sometimes appears by implication that they think God is rendered impotent when it comes to being able to do this) heal you from your past wounds;
- it is further suggested that it is quite simple to 'forgive and forget', and provided you manage somehow to 'forget' that you will then have managed to 'forgive' – as if finding the right formula with which to 'forget and forgive' allows God (or something else) to produce a magic paint-brush which undoes all the past damage and produces a clean start. The words 'denial' or 'repression' of past events are somehow not equated with forgetting!

We do not see forgiveness in such simple terms. We believe that the first two points of view contain some aspects of truth, each is important and neither excludes the other. It therefore seems to us that some advice given by well-meaning Christians and church leaders is not only inadequate from an emotional and psychological point of view, but sadly also has the effect of distorting the true nature of God's all-embracing love.

We do not regard forgiveness as bearing even a vague similarity to trying to pretend that there used to be fairies at the bottom of our gardens – by pretending that the painful and hurtful things that were done or said never really happened and that as long as some one believes hard enough they can create an inner world for themselves where they see only the fairy lights of unreality and not the darkness that the lights obscure.

For many survivors the human mind is past master at offering escape from some of the overwhelming feelings that go with memory of abuse, and the human mind unasked and of its own accord puts certain memories out of reach until such time as it is possible for them to surface and be dealt with, or until they can no longer be repressed for other reasons.

An essential prerequisite to forgiveness is facing head on the harsh reality and the darkness both of what was done and also those areas in which someone wishes they had responded differently. In the case of sexual abuse this means confronting childhood's realities as much as can be remembered and regained. It means reliving how it had been to be bullied, conned, frightened, ignored, intimidated, treated as a thing rather than as a person and so on. This may sound fine in theory but is hard in practice for most people, since as children they needed to trust that their parents and caregivers were good, and therefore when treated badly tended to deflect their anger onto other people or inwards onto themselves, rather than risk being enraged with the person who was supposed to be the nurturer. The idea of thinking about, of discovering and then of admitting, strong feelings of outrage and hatred about what was done and about the person who did it (or about the person who did not stop it) may seem unthinkable. But unless this is possible powerful feelings of anger, rage and hatred will be repressed and bottled up inside (like a pressure cooker with no safety valve) and these hidden, repressed feelings exert their inner corrosive effect, poisoning and warping both the personality and the body in hidden or obvious ways. It is only in facing such deep and intensely disturbing feelings that some survivors begin to glimpse the possibility of being able to learn how to forgive. Such hope springs from beginning to understand how it was that things happened as they did, of glimpsing what it was that might have made an abuser the person he or she was – their up-bringing and childhood and the past abuse they themselves may have suffered – of really starting to see things in a different light and even of discovering that there is room for compassion for the person who caused so much hurt. Sorrow and pain that things were as they were, and at the inevitability of some of it, may be part of this experience.

The process of Maggie's gradual discovery of a capacity within herself to forgive her father was rather like the gestation of a child: conception could be said to have occurred when she began to confront the paradox of her love for her father and yet her sorrow, pain and anger at what had taken place between the two of them. She writes:

> Crying, bleeding, membranes tearing
> I give birth to rage.
> Wrenching the thorn-embedded anger from the
>   overgrowth of withheld permission
> The labour lonely
> The grieving pitiable for a violation.
> Sometimes it seems the whole repellent history
> is a phantom
> and yet the pain is palpable.
>
> And through it all – incredulous, incongruent
> threads of forgiveness run
> spun from the love you gave so lavishly
> along with the abuse.
>
> And yet I did forgive
> and do and think
> and know
> you knew forgiveness too.
> How else could you have constantly proclaimed
> its ever-availability
> with so much freshly-minted passion?
> How else could I have heard and been so moved?

Some would see this kind of process in terms of true Christian reconciliation in which the estrangement between two people or groups of people is superseded by their coming to accept and, in some degree, to love one another. And the word 'love' does not refer to sentimental feelings, or to having nice warm thoughts about another person but rather to something made of stronger stuff, like setting one's will to work for the highest good of the other person. Someone can thus be loved while they are not necessarily liked. Ideally this is preceded by the injustice being confronted and dealt with. However in the world of the survivor of sexual abuse, this ideal, for many reasons, is not necessarily the best or only possible sequence of events.

Sarah was never able to confront and talk face to face to the father who sexually abused her for he moved to live abroad and died overseas. Monica's brother was so violent that she was too frightened of being physically battered ever to speak to him about what he had done. Stan's uncle, when confronted by Stan in his late 30s, flatly refused to listen to the accusations of how he had misused his nephew when younger, and the rest of the family colluded with him in keeping the whole thing under wraps. All three of these survivors were able to work deeply within themselves, with the internal image of their abuser they carried in their feelings and imaginations, over a period of several years to do the work of confronting their abuser that was a prerequisite of being able to forgive. Sarah went to her father's grave with a close friend and spent an afternoon there; talking, shouting, screaming and weeping her feelings about it all as if her father could hear her. Monica talked to a photo of her brother and made a tape recording, full of deep emotion and anger and pain, of the things she dare not say to his face, and entrusted this to her counsellor. Stan wrote a long letter over a period of several months to his uncle in which he remembered the incidents and the humiliation that had been his as a child, and then ceremoniously burnt it in the fireplace of the room where some of the abuse had occurred.

It was important for Mary, as an adult, to face her abuser and to say, 'I don't want you near my own children!' and for Celia to muster up the courage to say to the church leader who had abused her: 'With this between the two of us I cannot manage at present to worship in the same church as you – one of us has to move churches.' In her case it was the church leader who went – fearing that this adult, confronting Celia might reveal his secret to others.

In their own ways these survivors were following a pattern suggested by J. Houston[1] who says:

> While just reparation or punishment is not a necessary

condition of reconciliation, a readiness on the part of the offender to make good, so far as possible, the wrong done is nevertheless an important mark of his or her willingness to enter into a genuine reconciliation. Otherwise the costly grace extended by God or neighbour is cheapened.

For a survivor to be able to confront his or her abuser may be an important stage in reconciliation and in forgiveness but we believe that there are good and valid reasons why this may not be possible or wise in many instances following sexual abuse.

This leads to tension for some Christians since parts of the Church appear to offer such a dilute and weakened form of a cheap-scented commodity they call 'forgiveness', something so pallid and flabby in comparison with the real thing, that we sometimes wonder whether it can even be called by the name 'forgiveness'. For pastors and counsellors a problem may arise in understanding where forgiveness might fit in and in distinguishing between 'true' and 'false' guilt. Edward Stein[2] points out, that, among other people:

> Freud . . . distinguished between normal guilt (remorse) and pathological guilt and opened the way for the pastor and therapist to distinguish guilt that needs confession and guilt that needs therapy. Often enough these are intertwined, in which case both theological and psychological expertise are needed by the therapist/pastor.

When Lindy talked to her minister after a Sunday service about having been abused as a child, she was deeply distressed and in floods of tears. Her minister took her into the vestry, and fell into the trap many do when caught off-guard and when unaccustomed to dealing with such a painful subject, apparently wanting to get the whole thing out of the way as quickly as possible with as little distress to himself as possible. He suggested: 'Let's deal with this immediately. Let's pray and ask God to give you a forgiving spirit so that even now you can forgive that man and put it behind you for ever.' Lindy acquiesced for there was nothing for which she longed for more than to be able to erase some of the horrors of her past. The vicar laid his hands on her head and prayed. Lindy cried a great deal, the vicar went home to lunch feeling he had been of real help to someone that morning, and Lindy discovered a couple of weeks later that all her hurt and resentment were still there – but her feelings were now heightened by her new sense that the vicar had cheated on her by offering something that hadn't worked, that God was not to be trusted either and that she must be much worse inside than she had ever contemplated.

It is not, in our opinion, the simple matter it is sometimes made out to be by some of those gospel evangelists or pastoral workers who seem to teach about being able to forgive and of being forgiven by picturing a God who offers access to a kind of magic which works like this, so it is claimed: 'sin is like a cloud that separates people from God, and praying for forgiveness in the Name of Christ for all specified and unspecified "sinfulness" on the part of the pray-er then guarantees immediate access to God and a special relationship of being God's adopted child in this life and gives an entry pass to heaven in the future'. Partial truths have, we believe, been declared and distorted by such suggestions, and greater truth obscured.

The picture is much less simple for Alwyn Marriage[3] who suggests that forgiveness may not be experienced initially but rather later once there has been a setting free from the things that blind, cripple and bind. She says that:

> The hinge between what we are freed from and what we are freed into is forgiveness. On the one hand, we are freed from sin because we are forgiven completely and irrevocably by God. On the other, we are freed to enter into life in the Spirit, to live holy lives, but we can only begin to do this when we learn to forgive.
>
> In other words we are freed *from* fear, *to* love, *through* forgiveness . . .

The saying goes that 'to err is human, to forgive divine' and most people discover that forgiveness that is more than superficial verbal assent is something rarely produced to order. Some stay in their prison cell of bitterness, resentment and hatred. Some find inner resources, spilling out and enabling them to forgive. Yet others find they are able to ask for God's help in getting out of this particular maze. For some their guide is a counsellor, therapist, priest, minister, pastor, friend or relative, and for others it is something which the Holy Spirit works unexpectedly with no apparent human assistant. For some the sheer warmth of feeling loved and accepted by God melts the ice of unforgivingness and the freezing bonds of bitter resentment loosen, allowing something to emerge that has the appearance of early and developing love. Martin Luther King captured the essence of the end result of this in these amazing words: 'We shall match your capacity to inflict suffering with our capacity to endure suffering . . . do to us what you will and we will still love you.'

For Muriel it was a combination of all these factors. She writes: "There has never been a precise moment when I made a conscious decision to forgive my abuser. It kind of crept up on me unawares – through my work in therapy, my poetry, discovering my own inner resources and self-esteem and, not least, through an ever deepening relationship with God and feeling so loved and affirmed by God. But there was a moment when I had some kind of conscious recognition that somewhere along the way something had been changing at a more unconscious level. My abuse and my abuser were no longer an all-consuming, emotionally-draining factor in my life occupying almost every waking moment. Something had crept in unnoticed – an absence of bitterness, revenge, anger and resentment towards the man who so violated my body. I found I no longer wished to punish, destroy or to make him suffer as he had made me. I discovered that I no longer needed answers to all my questions. And to my complete surprise, I felt the first stirrings of compassion towards him.

"I don't know if this is what other people call 'forgiveness'. I think it has a lot to do with forgiveness – some will disagree with me. I own to feeling perplexed and angry when I was told that I must forgive my abuser if I wanted God to forgive me. What seemed to be wanted then was for the person talking to me to hear me say 'I forgive him'. But perhaps forgiveness is not as easily defined or understood as this. My own experience is that God sees and knows my inner soul and asks of me no more than I am ready to give. He knows my feelings, my ups and downs, my doubts, my fears and my search for inner meaning. He knows exactly where I am on my journey, accepts me just as I am and continues to offer what, in fact, he has never withdrawn – his unconditional love and forgiveness. I know with an unshakeable certainty and an inner serenity that I am loved and forgiven. No one can take that away from me or tell me it doesn't exist.

"But I'm now entering a new phase in my thinking about the meaning of forgiveness. Lately I've been thinking about the possibility of there being some kind of relationship between God and my abuser. Initially I wanted to deny any thoughts that God might love him too, nor did I want to have to share God with him. It was too painful to accept that God's unconditional love might extend towards those who cause us hurt and damage. Yet, the more I have pondered this, the more inconsistent it seems for me to want to be accepted and loved by God, dark side and all, and then to refuse to recognize that God's love extends to all people, including my abuser and his dark side – and what he does with it is between God and him.

"Those early stirrings of compassion have grown as I have begun to accept that he, too, no doubt brought the result of a damaged past into his adult life and relationships. This does not make what he did right or acceptable, but it does help me to understand a little better why. More importantly, it underscores for me that this man no longer occupies a highly significant part of my life and has no further power over me to hurt me or to destroy me, or spoil the growing self-esteem and serenity that is mine. Perhaps I may never be able to say the words, 'I forgive you!'. I'm not sure that it is quite this that God requires of me but I rest content. Knowing who I am today, and where I am today in this thorny issue of forgiveness is all I have to offer God and it seems, amazingly, that it is enough."

Forgiveness is something no one can attain by effort but is something worked out by some miracle (of God's) within the human heart. It is to be found as a result of heart-searching self-understanding, working through inner pain and anger, and, for some people, as a result of prayer. It is not something that appears to order nor can it be demanded from the pulpit, and yet it will not be made manifest unless a choice has been made to begin moving in the direction of finding the reality of forgiveness for oneself and of giving it to another. To refuse to forgive may be voluntarily to choose a form of emotional euthanasia in which one extinguishes the anguish that may well be the prerequisite of fully being able to live.

Forgiveness for Maggie was nothing to do with sentimentality or mustering and fanning nice warm feelings. It was about the agony from which her freedom sprung, it was about some kind of coming to terms with the past – which may or may not be labelled 'forgiveness' – and about the freeing of her inner self to fly. She writes:

The circle of recycled pain
the sum of her awareness
vainly she clutches hands to the offending and the
    offended hole,
sits on them,
gasping,
backed up against the bed-head,
knowing her 'No' will be the only impotence . . .

The assault passes
the dread subsides for now
the child
somehow
gathers her tattered self together.

The circle of present pain
  of barbarous thorns
presses and penetrates his brow
vainly he calls for assuagement
sour local vintage – yes
but God is not available
the suffering must be borne alone . . .

the assault passes
the deed accomplished
the Son of Man, of woman
commits himself
to his Father.

Blood-stained
circles of pain, imposed on each other
mutually contained
known most intimately in the hollow darkness
now in her thrashing rage
now in her sadness
the woman bravely
holds them to the Light . . .
and through them streams
a Presence,
glorious countenance
dimly discerned yet free from duplicity

and from the thorns
a rose blossoms.

And then Maggie writes of the hope that follows her confrontation of some of the bad done to her.

Bird –

carefully cleansed of oil and tar
released
from the sanctuary's hands
you fly again in the world
uneven, yet soaring,
my precious bird of hope.

and the sanctuary
remains open.

Rita Nakashima Brock[4] reminds the Christian of traditional faith and that:

> Believing that we have already been forgiven for our sin by a previous act of divine grace through the suffering of the Son can lead to self-acceptance and forgiveness of others. Being liberated from the fear of punishment produces an open graciousness towards others as happened in Luther's awakening to grace.

She stresses that this is but the beginning of seeking to right the kind of suffering built into our social lives, and sometimes made manifest in the abuse of power about which this book is concerned. Forgiveness must be revealed in ongoing action for it to have any depth of meaning and to be more than words and thoughts acting as a sop to quiet the conscience of those concerned. Righting injustice is a natural follow-on to the forgiving of a breach of justice in any form.

10

SENSITIVITY ABOUT SEX

Sexuality, along with spirituality, lies at the centre of each person's innermost being. The two are intimately linked and malfunctioning of the one usually affects the other. However, for years the Church as a whole has brandished placards labelled 'taboo' over any open discussion of the subject of sexuality. Thus, an influential group of people who major on spirituality have been effectively silent about an area of life that is vital to the well-being of all. Since the 1960s, society as a whole has shifted from Victorian prudery about sex to being more free and open on the subject. But, with some welcome exceptions, the Church has remained silent on this matter.

In some quarters, encouragement of discussion and struggle by Christians to find fulfilling and acceptable sexual expression appropriate for each individual has been stifled by the issuing of inflexible commandments said to be 'God's given decrees which must therefore govern sexual activity for all mankind for all time'. Thus, some state that 'unquestionably masturbation is wrong', 'genital sexual expression outside marriage is sinful', 'the use of any sexual outlets other than heterosexual penile–vaginal coupling is not right', and so on.

Within many church groups, people who do not fit the assumed or openly prescribed sexual standards of the group are deemed to be 'substandard' and feel themselves rightly categorized as second-rate. Thus those who have survived sexual abuse, those whose sexual orientation is towards the same sex, or those who are aroused sexually in unusual ways, may feel they have something within themselves that is inherently unsavoury, that needs 'confessing' and 'to be forgiven'.

This leaves many Christians struggling with the reality that their personal experience apparently falls short of the high ideals and expectations of the Church. It also leaves them without a forum in which safely to voice fears and problems as to how they can possibly manage to live fulfilled, creative lives in harmony with their sexual desires without being forced to compromise their integrity or to be over-secretive about their real selves.

This problem is compounded by the observation that it often seems to single people that those who pontificate the loudest, those who are the most judgemental and the harshest law-enforcers, do so from within the seclusion of their own apparently successful heterosexual marriages. That they have very little insight as to what it might be like to be single and living alone, or what it is like to have different sexual inclinations. Sadly, occasionally, such defenders-of-the-law have unacknowledged or unrecognized deep sexual problems themselves which may erupt into the light of day in 'scandals' in the Church or through revelations in the mass media.

If this area of life is difficult for many Christians, then it is exacerbated for those who have been sexually abused. Sexual abuse strikes at the very centre of one's being, damage to sexuality is inevitable, and is carried on into those relationships which involve trust and intimacy, love-making and sexual intercourse. A church that is perceived as being censorious, as making harsh judgements, as lacking in understanding and compassion for the diversity of the human condition may thus be assumed to have little to offer the survivor who is seeking to come to terms with a sexual identity that is already vulnerable. Some church set-ups, offering a framework of rigid rules, may appear to be (and sometimes prove to be) safe and containing for the survivor. However, such rules often do no more than bolster the survivor's defence mechanisms of denial and repression of fears and needs, and fail to offer healing and re-creation to that precious part of the personality damaged by the past.

We believe that ideally people should not live alone, that God created people with the potential to flourish through their relationships, and that ideally genital sexual expression belongs within the context of a committed marriage relationship. Would that life itself were so straight-forward. As a vicar we know explained in a recent sermon:

> The grave danger in the Christian life and in the Church's teaching is that because it concentrates on the ideal, and the ideal end of all things, it tends to forget about the every day struggle ... It's important to remind ourselves that our lives are poised between the ideal and the reality. We are buffeted by the two – by our own mood swings and body rhythms and by external circumstances ...

Reconciling high ideals with human fallibility and finding a middle path on which to walk forward with integrity are tasks facing the Church in areas relating to sexuality. Unless the Church does this with Christlike wisdom, sensitivity and gentleness it will fail – and it will certainly fail those survivors (and perpetrators) of sexual abuse in its midst.

Many church people are unmarried and may sense some stigma attached to their state – that of being a second-class citizen in a Church that emphasizes the family. Some may have a vocation to find fulfilment through celibacy. Others choose singleness in preference to living with a partner for different reasons. The majority have had no such choice. They have waited for the right person to come along, but by mid-life realize that time is passing and a committed partnership is now unlikely. Yet others have lost their loved one through separation, divorce or death. Many people who have been sexually abused choose either consciously or more often unconsciously, to stay on their own. This at once raises issues about how to reconcile high ideals about sexuality with the fact that to be human is to have sexual needs.

How can ideals about ways of finding sexual fulfilment and the facts of reality be reconciled? How are sexual needs to be met if no marriage partner is to hand? There are no easy answers to these questions with which saints, sinners, cynics, monks, 'women of the night', father confessors, sex-therapists, editors of pornographic material, theologians and philosophers have grappled for hundreds of years. We deplore those Christians who thoughtlessly trot out so-called 'answers', such as: 'God will be to you all that you need', 'Your Maker is your husband – the Bible says so', 'Just pray hard enough and you'll find that God will take away your desires – and if he doesn't that he'll enable you to control them', 'Do more work in the church and then your obsession with sex will go away', 'Get right with God, put him first and then your unhealthy sexual preoccupations will diminish'.

Often it is the silence in the church about singleness and its unmarried members, and within families themselves about their single relatives, that leads to all kinds of speculation and to fantasizing. Lynne explains what happened to her:

> Most of the women in our family marry and have children. It's plain that I was expected to stick to the family tradition. At family weddings I'd be teased or asked straight out whether I'd be the next or not? It seemed inconceivable that I'd remain single. But now I'm in my 40s, my singleness is no longer the butt of jokes. It's an embarrassment and has become the fuel for fantasies. It's not just the others whose imagination goes to town thinking about me – I find I fantasize about their fantasies. My fantasy is that they assume I'm a lesbian . . .

In the book *Secrets in the Family*,[1] the authors Pincus and Dare talk about the difference between those secrets which are based on facts and those which have no factual foundation but arise from fantasy. Both powerfully affect the person involved and the family unit as a whole, but it is often unclear whether it is the fact or the fantasy which wields the influential power.

Lynne continues:

> One relative did kind of ask me if I was gay, but he didn't ask straight out. In our family it's not acceptable to be gay but the truth about me – that I've had two heterosexual love affairs – is even more unacceptable and so I've allowed them all to think I'm gay rather than let them guess the truth.
>
> Sadly, the family doesn't know why marriage isn't an option. I couldn't talk to them about anything to do with sex and have never been able to. It seemed to be

one of those secrets that adults had about which children asked no questions. I'd never seen my parents express their love for each other, their marriage seemed unstable to me, and my mother often said that it was better to stay single than to have an unhappy marriage. Having no brothers I knew nothing about male sex organs. The only sex education I had was from my mother when I was eleven years old and about to start my periods. She said that I must never let a man touch my body and I must never touch myself as God wouldn't like it and Christian girls didn't do that sort of thing. She didn't explain the reasons for any of this nor the consequences of doing what she forbade. I received a clear message about sex and about my body – that both were shameful and dirty and that God would punish me if I was bad. This had far-reaching effects on my developing sexuality and on my sexual relationships.

But the tragedy was that my mother's message was even more damaging than might appear at face value. What she didn't know was that her words were five years too late for me. Since I was six years old I had been sexually abused by a family friend from my parent's church – and my parents hadn't realized what I was saying when I tried to tell them what was going on. Had our family been more open about sex then my mother's chat when I was eleven years old might have given me the opening to tell her that I had been sexually abused, but I couldn't say anything. I was terrified of being found out and of being punished both by my parents and by God for being so bad. My need to be loved by God and by my parents forced me to keep it a secret until a few years ago. This meant that marriage wasn't a viable option – I couldn't bear to be touched sexually and knew that since divorce 'doesn't happen' in our family there was no way out once wedding vows had been exchanged. So I live with the guilt of having the normal sexual feelings people have – but feeling that as a single person I shouldn't have them . . .

Many survivors share stories echoing some of the themes in Lynne's. Some have a deep-seated fear of men and of being touched, while others swing to the opposite extreme and find relationships tend to be sexualized and that they have many sexual relationships. Yet others marry but find that the past abuse complicates their relationship with their husband and the way they treat their own children.

Others, like Muriel, do not marry but may unconsciously select as sexual partners only men who are not on the marriage market. Muriel shares: "I never understood why I was afraid of a stable marriage relationship. My parents' marriage wasn't too wonderful an advertisement for marriage but it wasn't bad enough to put me off for life. It was only in therapy that I began to understand that underlying my fear of marriage was a terror of being intimate with anyone, a need to be in tight control of my own sexual feelings and responses, and a fear of being so committed to anyone that I couldn't escape from a relationship that, after all, might turn out to be abusive. Until this time I hadn't realized how much this part of me had been damaged.

"Since my first two boy-friends had come from the same church background as me it wasn't hard to stick to teachings that sex belonged to marriage. Then in my late 20s I met a non-Christian man who was divorcing his wife and who didn't share my religious beliefs. Sex soon became an issue between us – him for it and me not so sure. To his surprise, I tried to get out of it by saying things like, 'My family wouldn't approve ... the Bible says it's wrong ... my church wouldn't like it ... I don't want to risk pregnancy ...'. In the end I couldn't escape the realization that what was really stopping me wasn't any of these things, it was that I feared being touched and was repulsed by thoughts of sexual intercourse. I knew that such feelings were not normal. Other people made love. So, I learned how to be like them and to do as they did – to have sex. But it was a case of enduring rather than enjoying what was going on, and I did it so that my friend would accept me."

Muriel did not then understand that the abuse of childhood was warping her adult relationships. When her friend's divorce came through, she literally ran away from New Zealand to England without saying goodbye, unable to face the implication that divorce meant that marriage was now possible.

She continues: "I went to a large evangelical church whose teachings seemed to conflict with my inner reality. I felt guilty, ashamed and confused. Part of me longed for Christian marriage but another part of me sabotaged every possibility of this happening." Like some other survivors, Muriel unconsciously set things up so that she was deprived of the very thing for which she most longed – and the defence mechanisms learned to enable her to cope during the years of childhood were the ones that automatically came into play in adult life. She muses: "Hardly surprising. I longed for a loving, stable, sexually healthy relationship. Yet, how could this be mine when my first experience of sex had been such a betrayal of my trust and an unwanted violation of my body."

This pattern was one Muriel repeated: "Then there was another relationship with a married man – something that 'just happened'. He was safe for me because I knew I could always escape when I wanted to. There I was back with those familiar love/hate feelings about sex. Part of me loved it and responded. Another part of me blanked it all out so that my lover would like and accept me. I had learned how to play games all my life and played the game of making love well. We had a comfortable relationship that made me feel special, provided just enough sexual fulfilment, but left me free of any commitment. Therapy ended this! Returning memories threatened my emotional stability, nightmares and panic attacks dogged me. Making love became terrifying, especially when I was enduring flashbacks of what had happened during that abuse of years ago. I freaked at anything reminiscent of it – certain ways of caressing and touching now felt sadistic, were no longer pleasingly seductive. Suddenly my lover symbolized the one who had caused all those horrors all those years ago. I ended our relationship with no explanation. To the end I hid my inner turmoil from him."

Confusion about sexual intercourse is often also linked with feelings of antipathy towards the body. As Muriel says: "I'd never been comfortable with my body image. I'd always felt that a nude body was indecent. As memories of my abuse returned a loathing for my own body was unleashed. My body had betrayed me and I couldn't bear to look at it myself or have my partner see it." Some women survivors try concealing their female shape in trousers and baggy tops. Others struggle with their body by over-eating (producing a cushion of fattiness with which to protect themselves from sexual attention) or starving themselves into rake-like thinness (sometimes unconsciously wishing to have tight control over themselves and to have a body that is neither sexually attractive nor, once periods have stopped as a result of anorexia, able to produce children).

Muriel continues: "As I struggled to recognize all the damage of my abuse, my anger with my abuser knew no bounds. Among other things, he had deprived me of all I most wanted – a partner, a husband, children and a healthy sexual relationship. Such was my anger and hatred towards him that I sometimes felt I was going to explode. My therapist once asked me how I'd feel and what I'd do if my abuser walked into the room. My gut response both shocked and frightened me – all I wanted was to kill him. I didn't know I could feel so strongly and I was terrified at realizing how powerful and destructive my true feelings were. Yet, I was also relieved to find that when I actually opened my mouth and stated what I wanted to do that God didn't punish me by striking me dead, and that my therapist seemed to consider my response normal and appropriate. I began to be in touch with, and to work through the seething well of rage within myself.

"In therapy over the next couple of years I struggled with that precious central part of myself that had been so savagely violated and damaged. I began to grieve for some of the losses which should have been mine to enjoy during my childhood emergence into puberty, the teenage years of exploration and experimentation, and womanhood. I began to wonder what the future might hold for me and whether I was sufficiently healed to think of trying out a relationship again.

"At this time my former partner suggested that we should get together again, I took a deep breath and agreed. But this time I told him about my past and shared my fears and the horror of having flashbacks to childhood abuse when we made love. This time I experienced a man's understanding, tenderness and gentleness as we worked together to overcome the past in a present experience of caring love. This was crucial for my healing. My fear of intimacy in all its forms diminished. I stopped freezing inwardly, the panic attacks lessened and the flashbacks began to fade. I was now able to be an active, rather than a passive, lover and to express my needs and pleasures in love-making. For the first time in my life I enjoyed it.

"This was wonderful while it lasted but I have now grown and moved to a different stage in my development. What was on offer then is no longer enough for me. I am now able to believe that I am worth more than being another person's second-best and, although I don't know whether the opportunity for a permanent, stable, committed relationship will ever be mine, I am more able to live with not knowing and am more content to wait and see."

Through her sharing of such personal matters, through her making herself vulnerable in this manner, Muriel is expressing our belief that people are unique, and that God's healing is not prepackaged but tailored to suit each individual. Her journey towards this degree of healing was especially hers and the way she had to go. To those who would judge or deal harshly – stating categorically 'that this is right and that is wrong' – we would point in the direction of Jesus, that man of compassion and empathy, who wrote in the sand in front of the woman taken in adultery (John 8:2–11). Wholeness and healing are often about trying to find what is good and right in a given situation, and then running the risk of getting it terribly wrong.

Christian support may well be less about dishing up advice as to what, in the advisor's eyes, is right or wrong, and more about prayerfully entrusting an individual to the God of unconditional love who longs to save (to make whole) and to re-create out of the ravages of destruction. Muriel says that she "expected that God would punish me or stop loving me. But at this time I found instead that God was more loving, less judgemental and more accepting than I had ever thought he could be."

One important area of sexual activity that Christians, and others, find it hard to make sense of is that of masturbation. All kinds of nameless fears have been passed on from one generation to the next about the dire consequences of so-called 'self-abuse'. These range from unbelievable horrors (to the post 1960s mind) such as: 'You'll become impotent!' or 'Your teeth will fall out!' to the more plausible: 'It'll spoil your sexual relationship with your partner.' Children caught stimulating themselves may be told how bad they are and not only face parental censure but warnings of inevitable dire consequences. Since the subject is often taboo it cannot be examined in the light of commonsense or of normal sexual development, and so vague fears are perpetuated. Religious people readily associate this activity with the wrath of God and with doing something forbidden and sinful. In fact, biblical writers give no clear indication that masturbation is always such a bad thing. In the few instances in which it is mentioned it tends to be within the context of not squandering precious sperm needed to perpetuate the Jewish race (and this can be seen not so much as being a command not to 'spill seed' but rather as being symbolic of the uniqueness of God's chosen people in Old Testament times) rather than of forbidding for all time an activity regarded as inherently evil.

However, feelings of badness and guilt associated with masturbation are common, especially among those from certain religious cultures. Thus it is exceedingly embarrassing and difficult for some Christians – and more so for those who have been sexually abused – to talk about their own feelings on the matter.

Sally told us that although she did find sexual relief on her own and by herself, she felt so guilty that her daily prayer was that God would somehow help her to stop. Mary sighed with relief and said: 'Thank goodness I can bring this into the open with you. I thought I was the only person in the world who did this and that God would punish me for it.' Mike explained how he'd never forget the look of disgust on his mother's face when she caught him, aged eleven, fumbling under the bedclothes finding pleasure in his developing sexual organs. 'It's bad to play with yourself like that . . .' she'd shouted at him. From her Convent schooldays, Sheila remembered how the nuns, muttering behind their hands at one another, had hauled the children off to Confession if any of them were suspected of such activity.

But another male friend of ours exclaimed: 'What's all

the fuss! Surely everyone does it don't they?' Yet another commented thoughtfully: 'I think it's one of God's gifts to us Christians – don't know what kind of trouble we'd be in otherwise.'

Sadly, for many survivors, as we saw in Chapter 4, masturbation is something which was first learned within the context of abuse. Therefore feelings of shame, horror and guilt are associated with it which are carried into adult life. This shame is compounded by memories of sexual stimulation and moments of intense pleasure which may involuntarily have accompanied the abuse. Understanding that these moments of sexual pleasure were as unstoppable as the abuse itself, can be both liberating and healing, and can lead to an acceptance that masturbation itself may have both an abusive and a non-abusive pattern to it – and that for most people it is an inherent part of normal sexual development. Such sensitive matters need careful attention outside and within church circles, and cannot adequately be handled with clear cut and simple 'do this' and 'don't do that' statements. Enough harm has been done already without further damage being added.

11

BLOSSOMING SPIRITUALLY

Stories of how different survivors find their spiritual percep-
tion is transformed as a result of finding healing in other
parts of their innermost selves vary enormously. There is no
blue-print to spiritual budding, blossoming and fruiting.
This part of the journey towards healing is as tailormade as
are the other parts.

For Muriel it happened this way: "A sense of having been
betrayed is one of the most difficult issues I confront when
facing my own abuse. My parents and I were all betrayed by
the middle-aged baby-sitter whom we trusted. I felt that my
parents unwittingly betrayed me when they left me alone
with him and failed to see what was going on and to protect
me. The Church's overall failure to accept the presence of,
and seriousness of, sexual abuse in its midst has the ring
of yet another betrayal. Along with all of this I sensed an
utter betrayal by God himself. And this sometimes led to the
feeling that I, in turn, was betraying God by my lack of trust.

"I had always thought that the God I was taught about
who loved little children would protect and care for me, but
God seemed to have deserted me completely not only in
those moments when the abuse occurred but also afterwards.
In recent years, I realized how angry I was with God. How
could a God who knew everything that happened, who was
powerful enough to do anything he wanted to, and who
was supposed to be loving, justify having abandoned a little
girl like me to such a fate? Where was God when I was being
abused? Why hadn't God rescued me and stopped it from
happening? If God really loved me, surely he would not
have left me to a fate like this?

"Obviously, I reasoned, God didn't love me because I
wasn't worth loving. That was why he had been able to treat

me so callously. In turn, I felt that I couldn't love a God like that, no matter how hard I tried. But, strangely enough, I still went on searching for God to fill the emptiness inside me, and I now see that God began to show himself to me through those who walked with me on the different parts of my journey. Both the meeting of each significant person and the timing of each important event fitted in with precise, often unexpected, moments when I was ready and able to absorb the next element of truth I needed to grasp so that I might move on to the next stage of healing. This whole process had a pace of its own. At times I yearned for instant healing, for things moved and changed so slowly inside me, but I discovered that my spiritual healing went at its own speed just as the healing of therapy had. Sometimes I tried to accelerate the change myself but this seemed merely to slow it down.

"My religious background was one in which, at that time, retreats were virtually unknown. But I had met several people who had 'made a retreat' and the more I heard from them, the more the idea began to appeal to me. I found out about the different options open to me and, with my therapist's encouragement and much trepidation, finally landed up in Sussex at a retreat conducted by Bishop Peter Ball – who was then the Bishop of Lewes. Having arrived I felt totally out of place amongst the apparently 'super-spiritual' Christians there, and I silently decided to leave on the first bus out the next day wondering what ever had possessed me to try it in the first place. But then this monk-turned-bishop gave his first talk and I understood why it was that I had arrived at this place and was listening to this man. His opening words were ones apparently aimed at no one but me and my needs: 'It is only the shallow parts of God which can be understood. The deep parts are revealed,' he stated.

"I settled in bed that night in my small, simple room, having uncharacteristically removed the crucifix from the wall to hold in my hand, chuckling inwardly: 'God,' I half-thought and half-prayed, 'you must have a sense of humour after all ... for here I am ... the kind of Christian who thought that anything to do with Roman Catholicism was an "abomination" to you ... but here I am, not only in a Roman

Catholic convent but actually going to sleep clutching a *crucifix* – a symbol my past religious roots taught me was an unacceptable, heretical expression of the faith . . . the empty cross is what I'm used to . . .' But in the morning, when I woke weeping at the horror of the yawning chasm within me, it was that crucifix which symbolized the possibility that I might be hanging on to something more solid than the edge of the slippery precipice of oblivion or insanity – hanging on to something summed up in the words of a hymn that came into my mind in those waking moments: 'Nothing in my hand I bring, simply to thy cross I cling.'

"Later that day I talked to Bishop Peter. I shared how difficult I was finding it to reconcile God, love and faith with what had happened to me when I was abused. His loving acceptance of all my spiritual doubts and fears was unforgettable, as were his suggestions – firstly, that I should find a Church where I could feel safe enough to try to discover God through Christ and the cross by attending the Eucharist, and secondly that I should 'go slowly' with the Church. His words were music to my ears – the last thing I needed was an injunction to throw myself back into the life and soul of a church organization. Then, immediately, to my great shock he invited me to the following morning's Communion service. Hadn't he heard what I'd just said about my doubts and fears about God, I queried? His answer lives in my heart: 'God doesn't say "Come once you've resolved all those feelings," he says "Come with all those doubts, fears and anger." If you decide to come then I'll be privileged to minister to you through the Eucharist.' The service that followed was deeply moving and healing for me.

"By Easter I had found the kind of church Bishop Peter recommended, and used to slip in, needing to be alone and unseen, during the Sunday morning Communion service. At the first service, one of the hymns hit a raw spot within me in words about some of the things about God I found so difficult – finding in God hope, trust, protection and love. No matter how much I wanted to believe in the existence of a loving, true and good God whom I could trust, my experience of abuse rose as an insurmountable barrier and there seemed to be no way in which the two opposites could be brought together. Sunday after Sunday I wept my way

silently through the service in agony at my feelings of
dereliction and desertion, oblivious of others present at the
service. The vicar knew me well, understood my painful
journey, and accepted me as I was – never applying pressure
on me to pull myself together, to try harder, or to make me
believe anything at all. He simply reassured me repeatedly
that God was not in a hurry, nor was God putting pressure
on me to be or to do anything. He often told me that God
accepted me exactly as I was. Slowly the *possibility* that
God really might love and accept me, mess and all, began
to take root.

"Some of the hardest things for me to grasp were the
possibilities that God might have no conditions attached to
his love for me and might value me just as I was, that God
might not want a relationship with me for some selfish
reason of his own, and that he might not demand anything
in return. I had been conditioned down the years to feeling
that love was something that makes demands, wants something from me, and was withheld at times if I didn't live up
to expectations. I wondered, 'How can *God* possibly love me?
Me? I'm completely unloveable, damaged, scarred,
wounded, dirty, ashamed and frightened. There's nothing
in me anyone could love – let alone God.'

"Bishop Peter and I corresponded, and in one letter he
helped me begin to understand that it was more than possible that God might see beyond the mess into the inner
depth of my soul, and find me lovely. He mentioned a poem
'St Francis and the Sow' by Galway Kinnell – a poem which
touched me deeply. It talks about how it is sometimes
necessary.

> to put a hand on its brow
> of the flower
> and re-tell it in words and in touch
> it is lovely
> until it flowers again from within, of self-blessing;

"Soon after this I had a dream that was one of the most
wonderful and precious things ever to happen to me, and
which was a major turning point in my healing process. I
dreamt I was back in my home town, being driven around

my old haunts by a shadowy figure who turned out to be God. I told him where to go and pointed out landmarks along the way. We stopped in front of the house where I had been abused all those years ago and got out, but I was frightened of going into the house. The shadowy figure of the driver turned into the safe form of Jesus and he and I wandered around the neighbourhood discovering all my childhood play places. Then he took my hand and said, 'Come, it's time to go', and led me gently back to my old home. I noticed things long forgotten – the familiar garden, the cracks in the paving stones, the back gate ... till we reached the steps leading to the laundry room. I trembled, frozen with fear. I was now just eight years old in my dream and Jesus picked me up, held me close and whispered, 'Don't be afraid. I'm with you and I'll carry you. You'll be safe with me ...' Then he took me round the house and into each room in which I'd been abused. In the room where it had all started he stopped, sat down and held me on his knee, and invited me to tell him all about it. It was here that I confronted him face-to-face with the searing questions I'd posed so angrily in my poems and articulated in fury in therapy. 'Where were you when it was happening? Why didn't you stop it?' His answer was quiet and simple: 'I was there with you. What he did to you he did to me. I felt your pain – your pain was my pain.'

"I woke up at that point, tears streaming down my face, aware that something momentous had just come to me through this dream. I knelt in church at the Communion service the following Sunday, seeing plainly what God was saying – that God *was* to be found in the Eucharist, for it was through the cross that he had shared my agony. And for the first time in my life, the meaning of the cross became personalized. At the bottom of my pit of memories lay the wounded, tortured, crucified Christ who had already made my wounds his own. I understood then how it was possible in my experience for 'his wounds to heal' me. Nothing changed magically overnight nor was I totally cured, for a lifetime's conditioning in suspicion and mistrust takes time to undo. But God's love was beginning to be neither punitive nor demanding like some human love – I was being loved unconditionally."

Since first writing this chapter, the publicity surrounding Bishop Peter Ball and what some of the tabloid newspapers referred to as his 'sexual abuse' of a young man in his pastoral care, has surfaced. This caused pain and confusion for Muriel. She says: "When the news broke, I couldn't believe it. How could this be happening to this gracious, humble man of God who had given me so much in the early part of my journey towards spiritual healing? It must be a mistake. I knew better than to believe everything I heard through the media and knew, too, that the true story would probably never be told. Nevertheless, inevitably, I found myself wondering 'what if . . .?' and somewhat irrationally I began to experience familiar feelings of betrayal and anger for in sharing with him I had made myself vulnerable. Supposing it was true, where would it leave me? Could it invalidate all I had received from Bishop Peter earlier on in my journey? Could anything take this healing away from me or destroy my growing relationship with God?

"As I pondered these questions, I recalled feelings and emotions I had experienced on the day of my final session with my first therapist. The door shut behind me as I left him after our last session and I walked down the road in tears feeling I had lost something special, but in the middle of my grief and loss it dawned on me with a certainty I couldn't have known until we had finished seeing each other, that what I had gained in therapy was mine to have and to hold for ever. No one and nothing, not even the ending of this particular and special relationship, could destroy or take that assurance away. Similarly, as I wrestled with my feelings about Bishop Peter, I knew with startling clarity that the exploration of my faith, my discovery of a God who loves so unconditionally, and my spiritual healing (all of which had its roots in that very first retreat I made) could not be destroyed or taken away from me by the events surrounding Bishop Peter. The security of my spiritual journey lies in the fact that it is God through Christ who initiates healing. Bishop Peter, my therapist, my Spiritual Director, my friends are but the people God has brought into my life to share my journey at different stages along the way. Reaching this conclusion was just the beginning, for it led me into the thorny and complex issue of trying to understand the man who abused me. And as I've struggled to make sense of this it has helped me to remember that we all, without exception, have what Jung calls a 'shadow self', or dark side, which contains or represents all the parts of ourselves which we either don't understand, don't like or perceive as bad (that which we often call human weakness). Much of my therapeutic journey has been about trying to own and integrate my 'dark side' and, indeed, discovering that God loves and accepts me just as I am. I have puzzled over how to balance this with the high hopes and expectations we have of our clergy, church leaders and people who are in a special position of trust. When they get it wrong it causes damage, grief and sadness. I don't have the answer but acknowledge that if, as I am discovering, God loves unconditionally, then this has to include even those we perceive to have 'failed'. I have difficulty extending this to include the man who abused me as a child. If I'm honest, I want God to love me, but not him. He does not deserve God's love.

"But then, which of us does? For the first time I am entertaining the possibility that God loves him too, unpalatable as that may seem. This does not mean I condone or excuse what he did, but it does mean that I can begin to feel that I can let go of my feelings of anger and revenge, and trust God to act fairly and with justice. This has been very freeing and healing.

"So I'm glad to have had to think this through – putting my faith to the test as it were. Nothing happening now will ever change what I have experienced and gained. It is solid and dependable. Bishop Peter will always hold a special place in my heart for the precious gift he gave me in introducing me to the mystery of a God whose depths cannot be fathomed but who chooses to enter into and share every human experience of man through the mystery of the cross, of a God who not only loves me unconditionally but sees me as lovely. This message is one about which we all need to be reminded. Like the sow in the poem, it is sometimes necessary to 're-teach a thing its loveliness . . . and re-tell it in word and in touch it is lovely . . .'. This, of course, is God's message to every wounded and broken soul – and which of us doesn't need to hear it?

"I don't spend much of my time away on retreats, but

have found they offer beauty, peace, serenity and a spiritual haven into which to escape when I feel particularly buffeted. Shortly after the dream, I was staying at a retreat house in West Malling, Kent, reading a book which I intended to finish there. I had reached a chapter about the difficulty we survivors have in giving and receiving love, and about our problems in believing and feeling that we could or might be loveable. The words of that chapter began to prize open old wounds, my distress erupting afresh as I struggled to hold on to the sense that I could be loved and that God loved me. I went to bed exhausted from my tears and needing somehow to re-focus my attention on God. I had brought a tape by the author Joyce Huggett about prayer, had no idea what was on it but decided to give it a try to see if it could help me sleep. I lit a candle, held my crucifix, and turned on my cassette player, assuming that at best I might find some slight temporary comfort. Half-way through the tape, as I was about to switch it off and go to sleep, Joyce said words to the effect that she would read some Bible verses slowly three times and:

> to expect that as you hear them read, one verse or phrase or maybe a single word or pen picture will attract you to itself. When it does, switch off the recorder and write down the words or repeat them over and over to yourself so that you are receiving the message into your mind and into your heart – into the core of your being.

I listened, wondering what this was about.

"She read these words from Isaiah 43:

> This is what the Lord says. He who created you. He who formed you. 'Fear not I have redeemed you, I have summoned you by name. You are mine. When you pass through the waters I will be with you. When you pass through the rivers they will not sweep over you. When you walk through the fire you will not be burned. The flames will not set you ablaze. For you are precious and honoured in my sight and I love you. Do not be afraid for I am with you.'

I knew these words already but that night it was as if I were hearing them for the first time. I was overwhelmed by them.

The words applied partly to my dream and to my survival
and to God's presence with me. But the words that homed
in on my heart were the ones in which God told me that
'you are precious in my eyes and honoured and I love you.
Don't be afraid, I have called you by your name . . . you are
mine'. I started to weep again – this time in joy and wonder.
Sleep evaded me again for now I had to share with God my
overwhelming feelings. I did as Joyce Huggett had suggested
and turned my feelings into this prayer poem.

> Be still my soul
> and know your God
> within.
> > I long to love and trust you,
> > but find it hard to see
> > how you, or any other,
> > could possibly love me.
> > Or how see me as lovely?
> > That's quite another thing!
> > Tears of pain and grief
> > flow from deep
> > within.
> Be still my soul
> and know God's love
> within.
> > I bring to you my pain and tears,
> > my heartache and my grief.
> > Tossed about by doubts and fears,
> > my times of unbelief.
> > So many issues unresolved,
> > but this is what I bring.
> > Can you accept and love me
> > just as I am
> > within.
> Be still my soul
> and hear God's voice
> within.
> > In the stillness of my night
> > you whispered in my ear:
> > 'You are precious in my sight
> > and I love you. Do not fear.

I have called you by your name,
you are mine.
Be not afraid.
I am here.
within.'
Be still my soul
and worship God
within.
As Mary bathed your feet with tears,
loved you and adored.
So through my tears I bring to you
my gift of love outpoured.
You hold me close, my soul is stilled,
I know your words are true.
And in your ear I whisper back
'God I love you too'."

12

SURVIVING CHURCH

Joanne lowered her eyes to the floor, crossing her jean-covered legs tightly together, and began to share part of her story:

> It's in church that I often find things hardest. The people leading the service are nearly all men, the priest tells us what to do and what not to do, and when it's my turn to take round the chalice at the Communion service I nearly die of fear every time. They've said I mustn't wear trousers or jeans but a skirt for doing that – and the presence of all those men makes the vulnerability of wearing a skirt almost intolerable. I guess it's all to do with men and authority, and my father and his abuse of me when I was little . . . but I can't tell them why I need to wear trousers in church – I'm terrified . . . but I don't want to have to exclude myself from serving in church because that's really important to me . . .

The theme of problems at church was taken up by Sally, who asked what seemed like a simple question, getting an answer that was more than she had bargained for: 'How is it for you calling God "Father"?'

Joanne replied 'Often that's the bit I can't swallow . . .', she went greenish, gulped, looked confused and continued:

> I guess I might as well say it all . . . the whole thing gets to me sometimes . . . the having to put Jesus in your mouth at Communion . . . I feel sick sometimes . . . like my father making me open my mouth so that he could 'come' inside me . . . and having to swallow afterwards . . . The thought of another man getting that

> close inside my mouth is horrible sometimes . . . some-
> times I seem able to forget . . . but at other times I can't
> and when it's bad it feels as if I'm being raped all over
> again but this time with the priest pushing that stiff
> Communion wafer into me . . .

Sally was silent for a long time not knowing how to respond.
'I didn't know it was that bad for you . . . I'm really sorry,'
she finally said, and after a few minutes went on to share
her feelings:

> I think for me it's any authority figure that spells
> trouble. 'She' used to know what was happening to me
> and didn't do anything to stop it. When I asked her
> years later, my mother said she let him do it to me
> because that way it saved my sisters. So, calling God
> 'Father' feels frightening but when people suggest I
> could try thinking of God as 'mother' that doesn't help
> either . . . one parent abused me sexually and the other
> knew and allowed it . . .

The language and imagery used for God can pose significant problems for the survivor of sexual abuse – and the
Bible and the Church tend to use traditional language, albeit
understandably, without serious reflection as to the reaction
it may cause in a survivor. In Sunday school classes a child
who is being abused sexually may hear God referred to in
terms of being male, dominant, authoritative and powerful
(king, ruler, monarch and lord). Teachings about a loving
heavenly Father who good Christian children ought to 'love,
trust and obey' may present a warped image of God to the
child who has to submit to his or her own father's sexual
desires, and who may find herself or himself sometimes
actually welcoming this little bit of human warmth and comfort offered in an otherwise emotionally bleak world.

Images of God as being like a brother or lover are biblical
enough but open to serious distortion in the mind of a
child, or some adults, where a brother has been a sexual
partner. Such distortions tend to carry conscious or unconscious feelings which then become part of the adult who
develops from the child.

It was when Freda, in her mid–30s, was on an eight-day

Ignatian retreat that she remembered for the first time in graphic flashbacks how her father had abused her as a little child. Her Retreat Director had suggested that she should study and pray parts of the Song of Songs. As she did this the words and images began sexually to excite then to repulse her; instead of drawing closer to God as a heavenly lover she wanted to get as far away from this God as she could. The words about breasts being beautiful and about the smell of the body being sexually arousing made her feel sick. Then at night the flashbacks began with a nightmarish quality and she remembered with horror and terror what she had forgotten – that her father (a vicar) had often spoken to her in this kind of language. She was unable to tell her Retreat Director (a male priest) what was happening to her, clammed up, and only years afterwards talked to a nun about it all.

Where caring adults have abused the trust of a child it is probable that this child will develop into someone who has difficulty in establishing caring, trusting adult relationships. God, who is presented as being the greatest care-giver of all, may thus be the one it becomes hardest to trust. Mary worked in therapy for a couple of years, sitting in a chair face to face with her therapist. It wasn't until she first lay down on the couch, curled up in the foetal position, and felt herself to be the little child she had once been, that she found herself frighteningly in touch with her profound distrust of any woman in a nurturing role. Over slow painful weeks it emerged that her mother would punish her violently when she was little, then banish her upstairs, but later that same evening would cuddle up close to her in bed where some kind of 'love' was exchanged through genital stimulation. Eventually, Mary had escaped from this into religion and into God, part of her unconsciously hoping that here was a care-giver who was powerful enough to look after her properly and to protect her from her parents and her alien environment. But even this had failed. It was only in a one-to-one relationship with a female therapist that she was able to see that being unable to trust either parent had led to her understandable inability to trust the ultimate care-giver – God. The thought that there was a God who knew everything about her and who would penetrate every part of her secret being, sneaking up on her unawares, was as terrifying as her childhood attempts to hide herself from the parents who might find her, hurt her and then abuse her.

On the other hand, other survivors of abuse find strength and refuge in the understanding that a different kind of parenting may be found in God – in God they may find a father who really knows how to father, or a mother whose milk-filled breasts never run dry and who shelters her young under her wings. Alan was unable to model himself as a man on the father who used him sexually during his early teenage years. Conversion to Christianity gave him a profound sense that there was a male personality in existence somewhere (whom he called 'God') who was so totally different from his own pathetic father that he could give his whole life to this God, try to model his own parenting on God as revealed in the Bible, and go into full-time Christian service. But he never took his own children to meet his father.

Perhaps the Jesus who wept with grief at Lazarus's tomb (John 11:33) and who then 'snorted with fury like an angry horse', turns in compassion with tear-filled eyes towards the perpetrator of abuse (who may well be repeating what was done to him or her in childhood). But at the same time this Jesus utters hard-hitting words, in tones of judgement, on anyone who causes a child to stumble, declaring that such a person deserves to have a great stone tied round their neck and be drowned (Matt. 18:2–6). Finding a balance between rightful compassion and rightful indignation – between love and justice – comes hard to the average Christian, who is likely to finish up ignoring the whole subject of sexual abuse and its relation to Christianity and church life because it is painful to consider in depth and because there are few easy solutions to the difficult problems posed.

Reflection on some of the theories about a child's spiritual development throw up further questions for those seeking to share faith with abused children, or with adults who were used sexually as children.

Study of children's pictures of God fifty years ago[1] seemed to indicate that eight to ten-year-olds understood the attributes of God (what God is like) but experienced God as being distant and remote; eleven to fourteen-year-olds portrayed God in personal terms; while the fourteen to sixteen-year-old age group revealed internalized perceptions of God coupled at times with indications of doubt and fear about God.

By 1976 Fowler, a developmental psychologist, had put forward his structural-developmental approach to the development of spirituality which paralleled Piaget's stages of cognitive development and Kohlberg's stages of moral development. He suggests that progression takes place from a four-year-old's beliefs (which are filled with fantasy and fuelled by adult beliefs) to those of an eight-year-old (who accepts literally and at face value rituals, symbols and stories which show God as being a benevolent and just monarch). By puberty, the influence of school, family friends, television and so on, will have enabled the young person to broaden out so that he or she no longer sees themselves as personally living at the centre of the universe but as being part of a larger whole.

Gordon Allport[2] sees similar such spiritual development. A little child's belief system is governed by 'egocentricism, magical thought and anthropomorphism'. This comes out in the child seeing itself as the centre of everything and may be expressed in ways like: 'I was very bad and told an untruth. So, God has to punish me for lying, and that's the reason why my brother's doing all these bad things to me . . .' Alternatively, God may be envisaged as a kind of conjurer who will wave a magic wand and make everyone come out of his magical hat as doves instead of snakes. Thus, in the child's fantasy world, the abusive family situation may be transformed by God into a family life-style as innocuous as television's 'The Waltons'. Alternatively, some kind of compromise may be reached through, on the one hand, a mish-mash confused merging of teaching received about God, with the opposites encountered in daily experience. Thus the God the child is taught about who is omnipotent is merged with the father who is very powerful. When this strong father abuses the child in some way this may then have the potential in a child's inner, unconscious world, for equating God with an abuser. Allport stresses the difficulty a child may have in reconciling these things that are apparently contradictory. Thus, like oil and water, the statement that 'God is good and God is my father' does not readily mix with the reality that 'My Daddy is strong and hurts me and I'm scared of him sometimes'. A child's inner world may contain expressed or unexpressed feelings that either 'God isn't my father' or 'I've got to be a really bad person to have made these things happen . . .'

By teenage years, the normal adolescent's search for some kind of religious experience may be complicated not only by the usual rebellion against parental authority but also by how that authority did or did not react if sexual abuse occurred when the child was younger. Rejection of parental religious values may lead to normal guilt feelings but these may be compounded if guilt at being the survivor of an abusive situation is already present.

For many survivors of sexual abuse the fundamentalist end of a belief system – and our particular experience is among those at the fundamentalist end of the evangelical Christian spectrum – proves attractive. There is a church structure in which authority wields power, in which that authority is commonly male, in which authority is supposedly benign and should it be malevolent then there is a conspiracy of silence to keep the secret in the family (but this is done in the name of 'protecting the honour of God and of his truth'). Thus, when Sarah told her church elders that the minister was touching her up and feeling right up her skirts when she was washing up the coffee cups after services, she was told that she 'mustn't say wicked things like that about such a good man' and her words were ignored. The subject was so taboo that it could not even be talked about, acknowledged as a possibility (however remote) and brought out for investigation as to the truth and some straight-talking to the minister concerned.

Such a church culture has an intense 'family feel' to it so that members may even call one another 'brother' and 'sister', share possessions, and help out in ways common to relatives. Social life may consist not of parties and outings with friends but be confined to mixing with other church people in an endless round of 'fellowship groups', prayer meetings, Bible studies and 'church socials'. In its place this is well and good but at its extreme end, its rottenness may be seen in something that is incestuous – incestuous in a mild form where preference is given to choosing 'one of us' for a job rather than an 'outsider', or at a dangerous extreme that leads to abuse and genital expression between a figure in authority and someone under him or her and thus in his or her pastoral care. The young person, unconsciously attracted to such a church culture because it has a familiar feel to it, like that of home, may find themselves in a church culture that has hidden or overt abusive layers to it. For those women used to being in a home where women are subservient and are accustomed to being abused, such a culture may initially feel safe and attractive. After all, the authoritarian structure seems safe and harmless – as it often is. It is not until later that some may realize that they have joined the wrong kind of church structure for the wrong reasons and then need to exert immense effort to break free, sometimes losing their faith and their God in the process.

The evangelical catch-phrase 'let go and let God' may well ring with undertones of letting an abusive authority do what it will with you. It reminded Jean of being forced to lie back on the settee, and of allowing her mind to distance itself from her body while her uncle used her sexually. His sheer masculine strength pitted against her childish body meant that the only way out for her was for her to let go of the controlling part of herself, the part that wanted to object, and then to let him do as he wanted with her. That anyone should suggest that God might want something similar from her posed problems. She could not tell anyone about the fear that gripped her each time she heard the words 'let go and let God' for she assumed that no one could understand, or that if they did she would be shunned for her past.

Alternatively, a God who is extremely judgemental and severe may be the kind of God that such a teenager opts for – a God for whom there are strict moral absolutes, and for whom right and wrong are very clear. Thus the teenager may see himself (or herself) as 'a wicked miserable sinner in need of salvation' and either himself or both him and his abuser as totally deserving God's judgement and severest punishment – even to the extent of being destined after death for the searing fires of hell.

Messages from some pulpits hit hard to some survivors of abuse. From the fundamentalist end of the spectrum comes the hell-fire-and-damnation message, in which the woman (Eve) is usually held responsible for the 'fall' of the man (Adam). This is carried over in such teaching as: 'It's the woman's responsibility to control the man and not to lead him on, she must be careful about her clothes and smiles, and she is responsible for not so kindling a flame of desire in him that he cannot but have sexual intercourse.' This kind of teaching declares, often implicitly, to some women that 'The buck stops here!' with them. It might indirectly be interpreted as proclaiming that men are so weak-willed, so driven by instincts and at their mercy that they cannot do other than find some kind of sexual expression whenever they are aroused. Most men would strongly object to being seen in such a light! Such teaching hooks into the feelings of some survivors that they are the guilty ones – that their five-year-old seductiveness and sinfulness brought it to pass. They identify with Eve who handed the apple to poor Adam who bit it. Thus, the male, powerful God is readily seen as one who must judge and condemn her. One solution to this for some women is to follow a package which may be presented to her, labelled 'The path of salvation', and which she may welcome. To be saved from her past badness, her present sinfulness and to ensure that the future will be all right, not only must she follow the prescribed 'way of salvation' in every minute detail but she must also struggle to make herself completely 'sanctified' and totally the kind of Christian who is acceptable to God. She knows she has attained this standard when she is accepted by other Christians of this ilk. This means, in many cases, that conformity to set or unspoken rules assumes major importance in the life of such an individual. It is something over which she has some kind of control, which may help her deep feelings of fear of lack of control. But, sadly, she is thus subjecting herself to another abusive situation in which she is unable to develop her potential. She is now chained to a system which is supposed to offer eternal salvation and freedom in this life along with something called 'abundant life', but this may to an outside observer smack more of 'restricting bondage' than freedom to develop fully.

For the man or woman who has learned in childhood to be subject to abuse, to deny what happened, to keep the secret and to convince him or herself that things really are not as bad as they seem, the triumphalistic end of Christian fundamentalism offers a wonderful escape into a world of unreality which is declared real 'if only you have the faith to believe it is so'. This may at times turn into spiritual wishful thinking which confuses wishes with reality. Thus phrases common to fundamentalist evangelicalism, such as: 'You only have to believe God's promises for them to be yours in your experience' lead some to think that reality is the opposite of the truth confronting them. They are supposed to be happy and peaceful when really they are sad and furious – and belief is meant to be able to magic away anything other than pleasurable feelings. Thus, religion can be used to bolster defence mechanisms of denial and repression – and for some this may be the only way through a life that would otherwise be too painful to live. The words, 'Never give up a good defence mechanism, you don't know when you'll need it!' are timely for many of us – especially when it comes to us wanting to bull-doze our way through another person's defences to force them to see the truth as we see it. This can be dangerous. Until they are ready, caution and gentleness must be the order of the day.

However, all of this feeds further into unreality. Some ends of Christianity declare that once you have been 'saved' or 'born again' (believed in a prescribed manner) you are then 'secure' for eternity and what happens in this life does not matter greatly. It is the future glorious hope of a wondrous life after death which sees you through this rather gloomy existence. Resurrection life is thus seen in terms of something that happens after death – not something that can be experienced in the here and now of daily living. Thus, the survivor (along with many others) can file away all the bad things that happen in his or her inner and outer worlds, trot along to church, belong to the church ghetto community, not really engage with life outside church (other than necessary bread-winning activities) and spend life preparing for this glorious future eternity. The church itself does not have to engage with unpleasantries like sexual abuse – this can be shelved – for in eternity God will make everything better again so injustice, abuse and pain can be filed away, and preferably ignored by a collection of people calling themselves 'Christians' who sing lustily of their heavenly home, thinking little about the present world.

But meanwhile, in the present, Christian survivors like Muriel continue their journeys, sometimes helped by their churches but more often continuing regardless. Hope can be the ever present theme song for this journey.

As Muriel says: "Since the experience of my dream in which I, the abused child, discovered Christ was there in the pit with me sharing my degradation, isolation and pain, there has been an on-going awareness that I, the wounded adult, continue to discover him present in the midst of my moments of darkness – the black holes of despair into which I sometimes still stumble and fall. It isn't just that God 'allows' suffering and evil to happen to his children and then stands on the sideline offering hope and encouragement while we struggle to survive. If that were all it is, then it offers me no real hope at all. No, it's more than that! God, through the wounded, dying, risen Christ, is right in it too, mucking along with me, sharing the murky blackness and the muddied waters of my pain, those moments of despair and those times when it feels as if there is no hope of ever finding wholeness and healing. And because he is there, something changes.

"It is as though the risen Christ, through the cross, embraces my suffering, the evil, the darkness and despair and transforms it – transforms the sordid mess into something beautiful, a hidden treasure beyond value and price. I don't altogether understand the process, but I know that it is happening and in the recognition of this awesome mystery, God, through Christ, becomes for me, yet again, a whole new experience as I have discovered him, unexpectedly, to be at the very centre of my journey to find healing from the wounds of sexual abuse."

NOTES

1 Discovering Ourselves

1 (August 1990).
2 Hobbs, C. and Wynne, Jane, in *Lancet* (4 October 1986).

2 A Matter of Facts

1 Kempe, H., from Schecter and Roberg.
2 Rutter, P., *Sex in the Forbidden Zone* (Mandala 1990), pp. 1–2.
3 *Ibid.*, p. 22.
4 *Ibid.*, p. 7.
5 *Ibid.*, p. 21.
6 *Ibid.*, p. 22.
7 Miller, Alice, *For Your Own Good* (Virago 1991), pp. 281–2.
8 Silver, R., Boon, C., and Stones, M., 'Searching for meaning in misfortune: making sense of incest' in *Journal of Social Issues* vol. 39, 1983, pp. 81–102.
9 Stein, R. M., *The Incest Wound* (Spring Analytical Psychology Club of New York 1973).

5 Guilt and Shame

1 Freud, S., *Group Psychology and the Analysis of the Ego* (1921), standard edn., p. 18.
2 Macquarrie, J., *In Search of Humanity* (SCM Press 1982), p. 128.
3 Fox, M., *Original Blessing* (Bear & Co. 1983), p. 26.
4 Jung, Carl, in *Psychological Reflections: A New Anthology of his Writings*, ed. Jolande Jacobi (Ark 1986), p. 304.

6 Coming to Terms with the Past

1 Dominian, J., *Capacity to Love* (DLT 1985), p. 13.
2 Jung, C., *Op. Cit.*, p. 91.
3 *Ibid.*, p. 96.
4 Rutter, P., *Op. Cit.*

7 Burning Rage

1 Campbell, A., *The Gospel of Anger* (SPCK 1986), p. 14.
2 *Ibid.*, p. 61.

8 Heal with Anger

1 Rich, Adrienne, *Lies, Secrets and Silence* (Virago 1980).
2 Bass, Ellen, and Davis, Laura, *The Courage to Heal* (Cedar 1988), p. 129.
3 Deming, Barbara, *We Are All Part of One Another* (New Society Publishers 1984), p. 213.

9 Costing Forgiveness

1 Houston, J., in Campbell, A., ed. *A Dictionary of Pastoral Care* (SPCK 1987), p. 233ff.
2 *Ibid.*, p. 103ff.
3 Marriage, Alwyn, *Life-Giving Spirit* (SPCK 1989), pp. 98–9.
4 Nakashima Brock, Rita, *Journeys by Heart* (Crossroad 1988), p. 57.

10 Sensitivity About Sex

1 Pincus and Dare, *Secrets in the Family* (Faber and Faber 1978).

12 Surviving Church

1 Brown, L. B., *The Psychology of Religious Belief* (New York Academic Press 1987), writing on the work of Haims in 1944.
2 Allport, G., *The Individual and his Religion: A Psychological Interpretation* (New York, Macmillan, 1950).